Dedicated to the memory of the prisoners of Breendonk
and their families

Book design by YAY! Design
The text of this book is set in DIN Schrift.
Maps by YAY! Design

Note to readers: The plural of the German nouns *Zugführer* and
Oberarbeitsführer have been anglicized with an *s* ending.

Library of Congress Cataloging-in-Publication Data is on file.

ISBN 978-0-544-09664-6

Manufactured in China

SCP 10 9 8 7 6 5 4 3 2 1

4500529656

BY **JAMES M. DEEM**

with additional photography by Leon Nolis

THE
PRISONERS OF
BREENDONK

PERSONAL HISTORIES

FROM A WORLD WAR II

CONCENTRATION CAMP

Houghton Mifflin Harcourt
Boston New York

CONTENTS

CAMP OF TERROR: SEPTEMBER 1942–APRIL 1944

THE MANY ENDINGS OF *AUFFANGLAGER* BREENDONK: MAY 1944–MAY 1945

AFTER THE WAR: 1945–PRESENT

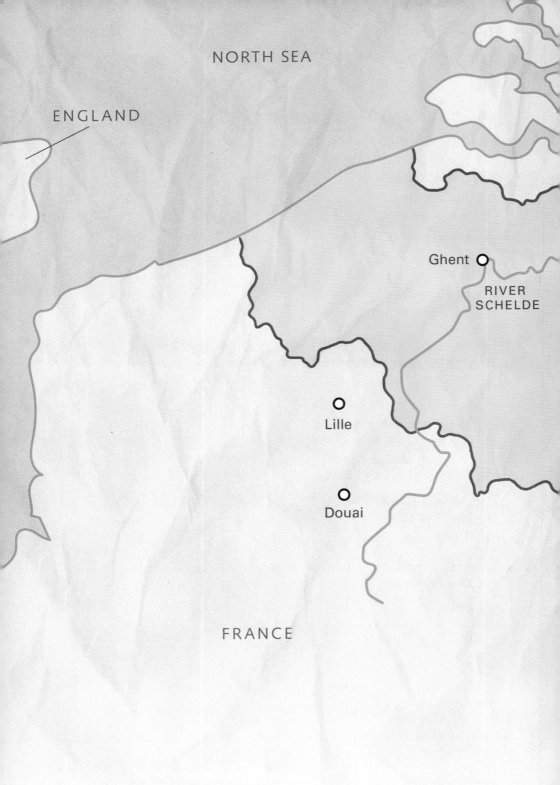

NETHERLANDS

GERMANY

Antwerp

Willebroek

Mechelen

BREENDONK

Hasselt

Brussels

BELGIUM

Huy

Liége

Charleroi

RIVER
MEUSE

Senzeilles

ARDENNES

LUXEMBOURG

Arlon

Plan of Breendonk, c. 1943

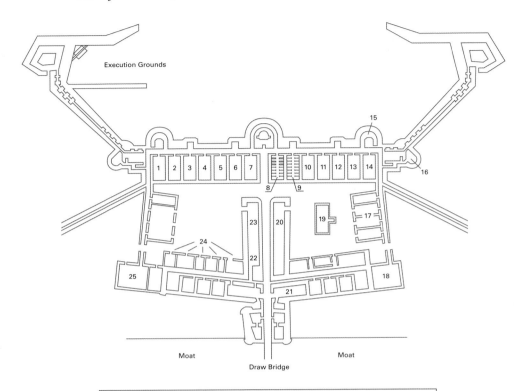

KEY:

Rooms 1-7, 10-12: Prisoner Barrack Rooms

Rooms 8-9: Solitary-Confinement Cells

Rooms 13-14: The *Revier*

Room 15: The Mortuary

Room 16: The Bunker

Room 17: The Jewish Barracks (built during the summer of 1941)

Room 18: Toilet Room (built by October 1943)

Room 19: SS Office for registering prisoners

Room 20: The Kitchen

Room 21: The SS Canteen

Room 22: First Solitary-Confinement Cells

Room 23: Tailor Workshop

Room 24: Pigsty, Stables, Blacksmith, and other workshops

Room 25: Shower Room (built during the summer of 1941)

DEFINITIONS OF TERMS USED IN THIS BOOK

ANSCHLUSS The annexation of Austria by Germany on March 13, 1938.

APPELL Roll call of prisoners, usually held in the courtyard at Breendonk.

ARBEITSEINSATZBEFEHL The work deployment order sent to 12,000 Jews in Belgium in August 1942 requiring them to appear at SS-*Sammellager* Mechelen.

ARBEITSFÜHRER A supervisor of the prisoners at work ("work leader" in German).

ARRESTANT (S), ARRESTANTEN (PL) A prisoner suspected of being a member of the resistance and therefore held in solitary confinement and usually tortured in the bunker.

ARYAN A pseudoscientific, racist term used by the Nazis. They considered Aryans—so-called pureblood Germans—to be superior to non-Aryans and later used this justification in their attempts to exterminate the Jews and Romany of Europe.

AUFFANGLAGER A "reception camp," a euphemism used to designate the SS prison camp of Breendonk.

AUSCHWITZ A Polish concentration camp with three distinct parts. Auschwitz I was the administrative center of the camp, established initially in June 1940. Auschwitz-Birkenau (or Auschwitz II) was a subcamp that became the "extermination center" in early 1942 with, eventually, six gas chambers. Auschwitz III was a series of at least forty slave-labor subcamps where prisoners were forced to work in factories or workshops, usually producing materials for the German war effort.

BETTENBAU Bed making, daily chore at Breendonk.

BUCHENWALD A German concentration camp established in July 1937 near Weimar.

DACHAU One of the first Nazi concentration camps, established in March 1933 near Munich.

ENDLÖSUNG "Final Solution," a Nazi euphemism for their decision to exterminate the Jews of Europe.

ESSENHOLEN Food server, a duty performed by some inmates at Breendonk.

FELDGENDARMERIE The military police of the *Wehrmacht.*

GEHEIME FELDPOLIZEI The secret police of the *Wehrmacht.*

HÄFTLINGE (S), HÄFTLINGEN (PL) The German term for a prisoner.

HERZOGENBUSCH An official SS concentration camp complex established in January 1943 in Vught, the Netherlands.

KRISTALLNACHT An organized attack, or pogrom, carried out by Nazis against the Jews of Germany and Austria in November 1938. The term is a Nazi euphemism that literally means "Crystal Night" but is interpreted as "Night of the Broken Glass." During this time period, Nazis and some ordinary citizens destroyed 275 synagogues, ransacked Jewish homes and businesses, beat and abused thousands of Jews, and were implicated in the deaths of at least 236 Jews, including forty-three women and thirteen children. It is also called the *Reichskristallnacht* and *Reichspogromnacht.*

MAUTHAUSEN An Austrian concentration camp complex near Linz, begun in August 1938, known for its infamous stone quarries and many subcamps.

MILITÄRVERWALTUNG The military administration that governed Belgium and northern France during most of World War II.

NEUENGAMME A German concentration camp near Hamburg, first set up in December 1938 as a subcamp of Sachsenhausen, then made an official SS camp in early 1940.

OBERARBEITSFÜHRER The head supervisor of the work site at Breendonk.

REVIER The sickbay at Breendonk.

SACHSENHAUSEN A German concentration camp established near Berlin in July 1936.

SAMMELLAGER A "collection camp," a euphemism used to designate the transport camp for Jews in Mechelen, Belgium.

SIPO-SD (*SICHERHEITSPOLIZEI-SICHERHEITSDIENST*) The secret SS police in Belgium, similar to the Gestapo in Germany.

SONDERKOMMANDO A "special work group" of prisoners. At Auschwitz they removed corpses from the gas chambers and burned them either in open pits or in the crematoria.

SS (*SCHUTZSTAFFEL*) The infamous Nazi defense corps that began by providing bodyguards for Adolf Hitler and became one of the most powerful Nazi paramilitary organizations.

UNTERMENSCH A "subhuman," a term used by the Nazis to refer to people they considered inferior, including Jews, Romany, Slavs, and other non-Ayrans.

WAFFEN-SS The military force of the SS.

WEHRMACHT The regular German army.

ZUGFÜHRER The prisoner who was the leader or captain of a barrack room at Breendonk. Similar to a *Kapo*, a term used in other concentration camps.

INTRODUCTION

My first view of Breendonk.

The first time I visited the national memorial of the Belgian concentration camp named Breendonk, I was shocked by what I saw and heard. Until that day, somehow Breendonk had escaped me.

I knew about the concentration camps that the Nazis had established to eliminate all opposition to their regime. Like many people, I had learned about the camps initiated by Adolf Hitler and administered by the SS before the start of World War II primarily to incarcerate those who opposed Nazi politics; they included Dachau, Buchenwald, and Sachsenhausen in Germany, and Mauthausen in Austria. I was acquainted with other Nazi concentration camps organized soon after the war began for political prisoners and resistance fighters as well as Jews and Romany; these included Auschwitz I, Neuengamme, and Dora. I was also well aware of the extermination camps, such as Auschwitz-Birkenau (sometimes called Auschwitz II) and Majdanek.

But I had never heard of Breendonk until that day in September 2010. Never designated an official concentration camp by the SS, it was labeled an *Auffanglager,* a type of camp where prisoners were held until they were either released or transported to other concentration camps. No matter what term the Nazis used, most people familiar with Breendonk during and after the war referred to it as a concentration camp. It was just as brutal and deadly, according to many of its prisoners. One man who survived Breendonk wrote that although the camp "had no gas chambers, no incinerators . . . Breendonk was no less notorious, no less a black hell of the most barbarous terror." Another claimed that he "would prefer to spend nineteen months at Buchenwald than nineteen days at Breendonk." A historian describing the concentration camp of Auschwitz I before the nearby extermination camp of

Auschwitz-Birkenau was built wrote that the camp "was widely known as a site of imprisonment, extreme brutality, starvation, illness, and high mortality rates, including killings by various forms of torture, shooting, and hanging." The same description

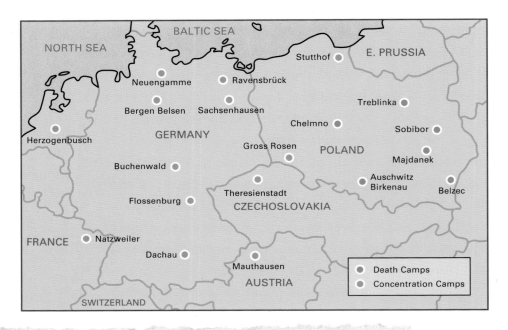

Main concentration camps and death camps established by the Nazi SS before and during World War II.

could be applied to Breendonk, only on a smaller scale.

Breendonk was not an extermination camp; only 303 of the 3,590 *known* prisoners died there from abuse, starvation, or execution; an additional 54 prisoners were executed at other sites. By the end of the war, at least 1,741 inmates had died, most after they were transported to other concentration camps. But these figures are incomplete, for researchers believe that there were at least 260 unregistered prisoners at the camp during the war, and probably more.

Although relatively few prisoners were incarcerated there

over the course of World War II—never more than 660, and that number for only a very brief time—its very smallness, "which made it possible for each prisoner to be 'dealt with' individually," turned it into a camp of terror. According to one writer whose thoughts were echoed by many others, three principles guided the treatment of prisoners: starve them, overwork them, and beat them often, "for no plausible reason."

After the war, some survivors wrote about their experiences at the camp. Because they had only *heard* the names of the others and because many different languages were spoken at the camp, they understandably made mistakes when they wrote about people. And so, for instance, Prauss became Bross, Obler became Hopla. Also, because prisoners were stripped of their names and assigned a number upon arrival, they often knew their fellow inmates by just a first name, if at all. Even then, the name Israel might have become Isaac in a survivor's memory. Because they were under stress, they sometimes became confused about dates: an event that occurred in December might have been remembered as having happened in March. No memory could be 100 percent accurate under such barbaric circumstances.

As I wrote the book, I took these errors of memory into account and corrected them cautiously. If I was not certain who was being referred to, I mentioned that. When it was clear who was being described, I filled in the blank. Still, I may have made my own inadvertent errors, and for that I take full responsibility in trying to tell this complicated story.

Throughout, I have tried to let the prisoners speak for themselves. The stories woven through this book are taken from autobiographies, interviews, archival documents, and courtroom testimonies. I have not invented any dialogue; every word that appears in the conversations was quoted from one of these sources. The only imagination I used was when I described what a prisoner might have experienced, and these suppositions were based on the writings of other prisoners. I have included photographs, often undated, of many prisoners as well, so that the reader can see their faces. But photographs were not available for everyone, especially those who died and had no surviving family. This was true of many Jewish prisoners whose families were deported to their deaths.

Students on a school visit gather around the photo of Israel Neumann, taken by a Nazi propaganda photographer in 1941.

As I left Breendonk that first day, I was haunted by the stories and the photographs of the prisoners that hung on exhibit in the dark and dank rooms of the camp. One image in particular stayed with me: a photograph of a man named Israel Neumann. It was his heartbreaking story that propelled me to learn more about Breendonk and its prisoners.

Since then, I have returned to Breendonk well over a dozen times, to work in its archives, to wander through its echoing deserted hallways on rainy afternoons, to study the stucco wall in the courtyard, to step into the torture chamber, and to stand in silence on the execution grounds. But I always come back to the photo of Neumann.

That is why I chose to begin the book with him.

HALT

Wer weiter geht wird ersch

Wie verder gaat w

doodgeschoten

Qui dépasse cette limite sero

September–December 1940

1

THE ARREST OF ISRAEL NEUMANN

The Antwerp Central Station where Israel Neumann was arrested in the early fall of 1940.

Israel Neumann was one of the first to be arrested.

One night in late September or early October, unable to sleep because his stomach was growling from hunger, he left his home at 20 Magdalena Street in Antwerp, Belgium, and went for a walk near the main railway station, intending to buy something to eat. Perhaps he had done this many times before, perhaps he felt safe.

But the year was 1940, and World War II had already begun in Europe. Belgium had been invaded by Germany and was now under the control of a German military administration, the *Militärverwaltung*. During his outing, Neumann was stopped by the *Geheime Feldpolizei,* the secret police of the German army, and detained.

No records of the event were kept; no arrest report was ever filed. The specific date of his arrest is not even known. But there is no doubt that he was taken into custody. His crime, according to one source, was that he had

Israel Neumann, 1927.

perhaps uttered something—a word, a phrase, a sentence or two—that was interpreted as anti-Nazi. On the other hand, the military police could have arrested him for what they termed a "racial reason." In other words, Israel Neumann's crime that night might simply have been that he was a Jew.

——————

In 1940, Belgium had an estimated population of some 70,000 Jews, only 4,000 of whom were Belgian citizens. The rest, like Israel Neumann, were immigrants, and many of them were quite poor. Some had arrived in the 1920s, mostly from Poland and other eastern European countries where poor job op-portunities and growing anti-Semitism prompted them to leave. Others had emigrated from Germany beginning in 1933, when Adolf Hitler and his National Socialist German Workers'

Party began to institute anti-Jewish laws. Still others had come from Austria in 1938, soon after the country was annexed by Germany in the *Anschluss*. Finally, another influx of Jewish immigrants from Germany and Austria occurred following the pogrom now called *Kristallnacht,* in November 1938, when Nazis and their sympathizers terrorized the Jews of these two countries.

Born in Nisko, Poland, Neumann had arrived in Belgium in 1927, but after a very different journey. He and his parents, three sisters, and two brothers had left Poland and made their way to France, planning to immigrate to the United States, where another son already lived. In January 1921, they sailed on the SS *Roussillon* from Le Havre to New York, incorrectly listed on the ship's manifest as the "Neumain" family. At Ellis Island, they were detained, although the reason is unclear. An immigration agent checked a column on the family's arrival form indicating that Israel Neumann was either "deformed or crippled." Immigration officers were always on the lookout for individuals who might not be able to support themselves and would require public assistance. Because Neumann was a man who may have had both physical and intellectual disabilities, his entry was at risk. Perhaps because he was accompanied by his family, all were allowed to enter after a short delay.

In New York, the family settled in Brooklyn, where they changed the spelling of their last name to Newman, and the children assumed Americanized first names: his sister Sima became Sylvia, his brother Meilech adopted Milton, and Israel was renamed Sam.

He lived in New York for more than four years. For unknown reasons, however, he decided to return to Europe, shortly after July 31, 1925. A little over a year later, in October 1926, he sailed back to New York. Upon arrival, he was placed in the Ellis Island Immigration Hospital for an unspecified illness.

After his release nine days later, he was detained and labeled "LPC PH HOLD." Immigration officials believed that he was unable to support himself ("likely public charge," or LPC) and that he had some mental or physical challenges ("physical health," or PH). The few existing documents do not reveal whether he was able to reach out to his family in New York City or, if he did, whether they tried to help him.

On February 4, 1927, after more than three months in detention on Ellis Island, he was deported to Le Havre. In May that same year, he immigrated to Belgium.

———

Immigrants at Ellis Island in New York City had to pass a strict medical inspection before being admitted to the United States.

Employed first as a waiter and then as a hotel porter, Neumann struggled to earn a living, as did many immigrant Jews in Belgium. Although the Belgian government allowed him to enter the country, he was still an outsider with no easy route to citizenship; becoming a citizen took considerable time and money, something that many immigrants did not have. Neumann's jobs did not last long. Eventually, he became a peddler. Licensed only to sell toys, he would hawk anything he could as he walked the streets of Antwerp in order to earn money to support himself and his wife, Eleonore Sabathova, but the police were on the lookout for any illegal activity.

Once, he was cited for peddling chocolate to innkeepers along London Street and fined. Another time, he ate lunch at a department store restaurant but could not pay for his meal. When the police were called, he told the responding officer, "I was hungry and had no money. I'll make sure I pay the bill." As a punishment, he was fined just over 17 Belgian francs.

But these had been minor infractions with minimal fines. This time, his arrest would have much more serious consequences.

Eleonore Sabathova, c. 1930.

After he did not return home on that early-fall night, a concerned Eleonore went to the police to report him missing. She gave them this description: "small size, dark eyes, lightweight overcoat, dark gray hat, striped trousers."

But the Antwerp police could be of little help, because he had simply disappeared with officers of the *Geheime Feldpolizei*. What Eleonore would learn later was that her husband had been sent to Fort Breendonk, a prison camp established by the Nazis the previous month. Although the exact date of his arrival at Breendonk is no longer known, it was most likely October 4.

On that day, he would have been trucked to the camp with at least nine other prisoners, most likely all Jews. Individual prisoners sometimes arrived in a private car: a Volkswagen, a Citroën, a Mercedes, or even a Buick or a Cadillac, according to some prisoners. However he arrived, the vehicle traveled halfway down the Antwerp-Brussels highway, turned toward the village of Willebroek, drove along a barbed-wire fence that encircled the perimeter of the old fort, and passed through a guarded barrier to a small plaza that also served as a parking lot. There, according to one prisoner, the detainees were "vomited" from the vehicle. Although the name Breendonk came from an Old Dutch term meaning "broad marsh," there was nothing picturesque about the place.

Surveying the entrance—a tunnel that seemed to form a gaping mouth in the concrete gatehouse of the fort—Neumann

The entrance to Breendonk.

would have tried to make sense of where he was. As an immigrant without much knowledge of Belgian history, he might have never heard of the fort before, but many prisoners taken to Breendonk—even well-educated native Belgians—were unfamiliar with it.

In the early months of *Auffanglager* Breendonk, few prisoners would have known that they were about to enter the gateway to hell.

2

BUILDING
BREENDONK

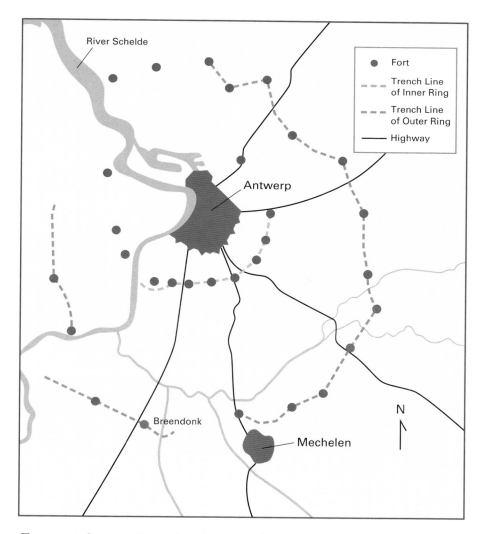

To protect it from attack by an invading army, Antwerp was encircled by two
rings of forts. Breendonk was positioned to the south in the outer ring.

One of a chain of forts that formed a defensive outer ring around the port city of Antwerp to protect it from a German invasion, Breendonk was constructed between 1909 and 1914. At least five forts followed Breendonk's architectural plan: a sideways-H-shaped body with narrow structures, called caponiers, extending outward from each end of the rear wing. Its walls, made from concrete and about eight feet thick, were intended to withstand bombardment by nine-inch artillery shells.

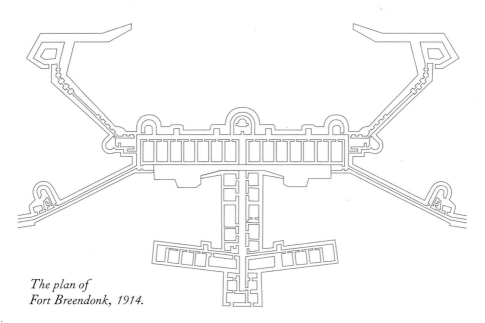

The plan of
Fort Breendonk, 1914.

The front, or north, wing of the H housed administrative offices and workshops. At its center was the only entrance to the fort. To gain access, a visitor had to cross a drawbridge, because the entire fort, like some medieval castles, was surrounded by a moat.

A dark, narrow cobblestoned corridor led from the entrance toward the rear, or south, wing of the H, the fort's strongest side; it faced away from Antwerp and toward the presumed direction of an enemy attack. This wing contained the barracks for the soldiers stationed there. On the roof above were a number of metal turrets that enclosed various large guns and artillery to keep the enemy at a distance. If that failed, soldiers inside the fort could use the small openings in the caponiers to fire at invaders during a close-range ground attack.

An unusual feature of the fort was that it was camouflaged, covered with a thick layer of sand excavated when workers dug the moat. All an approaching enemy from the

From the south (top of photo), an attacking army would have seen only sand hills rising beyond a moat and a series of domes that covered the fort's artillery.

south would have seen were a few domes and grassy hills.

By the time Germany invaded Belgium in September 1914, at the beginning of World War I, the defenses of Breendonk and the other forts had already been eclipsed by more powerful artillery with larger mortars. The Germans pounded Breendonk with a new short-range cannon nicknamed Big Bertha. Even though the fort had sturdy walls and was buried beneath tons of sand, it could not withstand the

This postcard, printed just after the end of World War I, shows the roof of Breendonk's south wing with its covering of sand and turrets still intact.

terrible shelling. Two days after the assault began, Breendonk capitulated, the last Belgian fort to surrender.

After World War I ended in 1918, Breendonk was used to store surplus uniforms and equipment and only occasionally

General Alexander von Falkenhausen, head of the Militärverwaltung.

to train recruits. But when Germany invaded Belgium in World War II, the Belgian army reclaimed the fort as its command center, because of its ideal location between the main cities of Antwerp and Brussels. By the time Belgium surrendered on May 28, 1940, after the brief eighteen-day campaign, Breendonk had been abandoned.

The fort would not remain idle for long; the German occupiers would soon find a new purpose for it.

———

To control Belgium and northern France, the German dictator Adolf Hitler chose to establish a *Militärverwaltung* headed by the *Wehrmacht* general Alexander von Falkenhausen. This military administration planned to keep the Belgian infrastructure primarily intact, allowing most Belgian civil servants to stay in their jobs rather than replacing them with German military personnel. In this way, the Germans hoped that everyday life in Belgium would continue to function as normally as possible without disruption. Factories would remain open, and their output could be more easily siphoned off to supply Germany with the resources it needed to continue the war.

Under this plan, the *Militärverwaltung* was supported by two police forces from the *Wehrmacht*: the *Feldgendarmerie* and the *Geheime Feldpolizei*. The *Feldgendarmerie* was responsible for policing German troops, cracking down on the black market of rationed goods, and locating Belgian workers who tried to avoid forced labor deportations to Germany. The *Geheime Feldpolizei* was its undercover police force that searched for resisters, saboteurs, and anyone who was "considered a threat to public order."

In June 1940, however, von Falkenhausen asked officials in Berlin for additional reinforcements for his police units. This request aroused the suspicion of senior leaders in the *Schutzstaffel* (SS) who wanted their own share of power and their own police force in Belgium. They did not trust the aristocratic von Falkenhausen and questioned his devotion to Nazi ideology. So in July 1940, the SS opened a large office in Brussels from which their police, called the SIPO-SD, could operate in Belgium. The SIPO-SD was similar to the Gestapo, or secret police, in Germany; in fact, the terms were used interchangeably by many people arrested in Belgium during the war. Although it was supposed to report to von Falkenhausen, the SIPO-SD, like its Gestapo counterpart, took its orders from the SS in Berlin. This often conflicted with the goals of the German military administration in Belgium.

The SIPO-SD soon requested its own prison camp to house "Jews and dangerous prisoners"; it did not want to place them in regular Belgian jails administered by the *Wehrmacht*. So von Falkenhausen proposed the deserted fort at Breendonk. Such an agreement was not unique. A similar arrangement had been made in Poland a few months earlier, when SS officials were searching for a place to incarcerate Polish political prisoners; they came across an old military barracks in Oświęcim and turned it into the first stage of a concentration camp that they called Auschwitz.

SS-Major Philipp Schmitt.
(Kropf photo 30)

By the end of August 1940, Fort Breendonk had begun to turn into what the SS euphemistically termed an *Auffanglager,* or "reception" camp. Although it was not officially a concentration camp, the difference in title meant little. The main purpose of a concentration camp was "the elimination of every trace of actual or potential opposition to Nazi rule." Breendonk was intended to house prisoners whose political views or activities were anti-Nazi. Most prisoners were expected to stay for a time. Some would be released, but others would be deported to camps mainly in Germany, Poland, or Austria. In a sense, Breendonk became the entry into the larger SS concentration camp system for many prisoners.

But to make certain that the camp did not overflow with revolutionaries and resisters who might band together and plan anti-Nazi activities, many common criminals were initially sent there as well. They included petty thieves, smugglers, forgers, and black marketers, as well as many Jews, such as Israel Neumann, arrested for no documented reason at all.

———

The house of Mr. and Mrs. Verdickt, 2013.

Selected to be the camp's first commandant, SS-Major Philipp Schmitt was driven to Breendonk by his chauffeur at the end of August. Schmitt, who had joined the Nazi Party when he was twenty-two years old and worked his way up through the ranks, was, according to his SS personnel file, "a good Nazi." His promotion to commandant at *Auffanglager* Breendonk was an important step in his career. But it was not fit to be Schmitt's home.

Instead, he knocked on the door of the house across the road from Breendonk: the Verdickt residence. Schmitt informed Mrs. Verdickt that he needed room and board. Although she wanted to refuse the SS officer, Mrs. Verdickt felt that she had no choice. Over the next weeks, Schmitt and eventually seven others, including his wife, Ilse Birkholz from Hoboken, New Jersey, moved in and took over most of the house, leaving Mrs. Verdickt and her husband only two rooms.

She was required to wash her boarders' clothes and cook them three meals a day. Given only a small allowance, she was told to provide meat at both lunch and dinner, an impossible task given the scarcity of meat—unless she purchased it illegally on the black market. Items such as bread, meat, flour, eggs, butter, milk, sugar, and potatoes were strictly rationed by the Nazis; even with ration cards, families often could not find the food they had been allotted, and many resorted to the black market. This often meant visiting farmers in the countryside or shops in their village where merchants such as beauty salons and florists sold black-market goods on the side.

Mrs. Verdickt, c. 1945.

Schmitt told Mrs. Verdickt to inform him if she had to purchase anything on the black market, and he would arrest those involved. Although she used the black market to procure enough meat, she chose to say nothing to Schmitt.

Three weeks later, on September 20, 1940, with Schmitt and his colleagues settled in, Mrs. Verdickt witnessed the arrival of the first four prisoners. During the first years of the *Auffanglager* Breendonk, she became acquainted with the men who were sent to fetch water at her house because the fort did not have an ample supply. Whenever she and her

In this photograph taken after World War II, Mrs. Verdickt's house can be seen circled in the foreground.

husband could, they slipped them some bread or butter or some meat left over from her Nazi boarders.

Only in 1944 did Nazi authorities ask her and her husband to vacate their home. Until that time, she saw what was happening to the prisoners at the old fort from her back window, but she was powerless to do anything about it.

3.

FACING THE WALL

The entrance tunnel at Breendonk.

A waiting Israel Neumann and his companions on the first October day of his imprisonment were the soldiers of the *Wehrmacht,* the guards at Breendonk and later the executioners. They greeted the prisoners with crude insults shouted in German.

Then Neumann and the others would have been marched inside—perhaps pushed and shoved along, perhaps kicked and hit with rifle butts and whips—through a large iron gate and down a narrow, dark tunnel. He would have felt a steady wind rush against his face until he reached a vaulted, open

New prisoners were forced to face the wall of the west courtyard. (Kropf photo 33)

intersection. There, incoming prisoners would have seen two large courtyards, one on either side. Small arriving groups were pushed toward the right, or west, courtyard; larger groups would have been divided between the courtyard and the entrance tunnel. Whether they were in the tunnel or in the courtyard, prisoners would have heard a voice order, *Gegen die Wand! Schnell!* "Face the wall! Hurry up!"

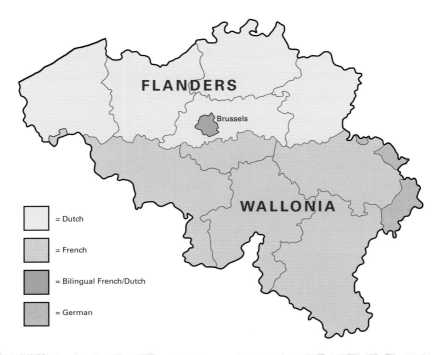

FLANDERS

Brussels

WALLONIA

= Dutch

= French

= Bilingual French/Dutch

= German

Belgium is divided into four language areas: Dutch in the north, French in the south, German in the east, and bilingual French and Dutch in Brussels.

All the orders were given—almost always screamed—in German; the guards and the SS officers would speak nothing else. Prisoners had to learn to understand German quickly, and once they were registered, they could speak only German to the guards. Refusing or forgetting to do this would bring brutal punishment. Neumann was fortunate, since he already spoke at least some German. But many arriving prisoners did not. Most spoke one of Belgium's two main languages: Dutch, the chief language in the Flemish north, and French, the main language in the Walloon south. Dutch-speaking prisoners had an easier time complying with German commands, since their language was linguistically closer to German. But any prisoner without a good knowledge of German was going to struggle with the unfamiliar orders at first.

The wall of rough concrete stucco that lined the tunnel and formed the back wall of the courtyard was remembered vividly by almost every prisoner who survived the camp. Most stood there for hours on their first day; a few claimed to have remained at the wall for days. A prisoner at the wall had to stand at attention—chin up, feet together, and arms fully extended down his sides, with the little fingers touching the seams of his pants—without moving. If a prisoner turned his head or shifted his stance slightly, he would be slapped or hit. The guards might use a truncheon or a leather horsewhip. Other times, they might strike the prisoner with a long, thin stick, which could cut into the prisoner's cheek or forehead with one slashing blow. If a prisoner moved too much, he might have his face slammed against the stucco. If he tried to wipe away the blood, he would be beaten again.

A prisoner soon learned to be completely motionless when facing the wall.

———

That October day, Israel Neumann most likely stood in the courtyard, facing the exterior wall of the prisoners' barracks rooms. The *Wehrmacht* guards would have marched back and forth behind him, their jackboots with toe and heel plates and hobnails clattering ominously on the paving stones. Only they knew what would happen next.

Sometimes they played a terrifying game in which one soldier ordered the others to ready their rifles and take aim at the new prisoners, as if they were going to shoot them in the back. Then the soldiers would pause. Time would pass slowly, uncertainly; the prisoners feared the worst. Fifteen minutes later, the command would be given to lower their rifles. The soldiers would then laugh at their cruel joke.

Next, Neumann would have been addressed by a

member of the SS. As commandant, SS-Major Schmitt would often greet the arrivals accompanied by his German shepherd named Lump, a trained attack dog. When he felt inclined, he

The SS officers from Breendonk pose for a photograph during the summer of 1941. SS-Major Schmitt is in the center with his dog, Lump; SS-Lieutenant Prauss is on the far right. (Kropf photo 21)

would encourage Lump to maul a new prisoner. But it was the responsibility of SS-Lieutenant Arthur Prauss, whom Schmitt had placed in charge of the daily operation of the camp, to speak to the new arrivals.

Für euch habe ich kein Mitleid, Prauss was often heard to say to new arrivals. *Hier ist es kein Sanatorium.* "I have no sympathy for you. This is not a rest home."

Ich sehe, ich höre alles! "I see, I hear everything!"

Short and stocky, with an angry and irritable disposition, Prauss was one of the inhuman terrors at Breendonk. One inmate described him, at first, as having an emotionless face, but he soon learned that Prauss's face was "expressive of depravity and cruelty." Prauss claimed to have been a guard for a time at one of the Nazis' first German concentration camps, Sachsenhausen, near Berlin. Although post-war researchers could not find his name on any work roster from the camp, prisoners at Breendonk who witnessed Prauss's violent temper had no reason to doubt his training.

Experience at Sachsenhausen would have provided him with knowledge about the procedures that would be followed at Breendonk: severe military discipline and hard labor. He was always seen carrying a pizzle, a flexible whip made from a dried bull's penis and woven with a metal wire, and he never hesitated to use it. He was also known to sneak behind a prisoner to catch him committing an infraction. The prisoners at Breendonk gave Prauss many secret nicknames, but the one that seemed most popular was Popeye, after a cartoon hero who seemed to have superhuman strength.

But there was nothing heroic about Prauss.

———

After Prauss's speech to the new arrivals, Neumann would have been made to wait longer—minutes or even hours—until he was called to the registration office in the center of the west courtyard.

An incoming prisoner was frequently part of a sadistic ritual that the guards and registration clerk repeated with zeal. When a prisoner entered the office, he might be hit across the face and pushed back outside because, he was told, he did not respond quickly enough. On his second attempt, he would run back into the office faster, but he might be beaten for failing to knock. The third time—after running to the door, knocking, and entering—he might be beaten for not asking, *Bitte eintreten zu dürfen?* "Please may I be allowed to enter?"

No one knows what happened to Neumann when he entered the office that day. His name would have been written into the registration book and assigned a number. From then on, he would be addressed only by his number; his name would cease to exist.

Then he would have been ordered to surrender his possessions. He likely had little to offer; other prisoners gave up watches, wedding rings, pens, toiletries, and any money they carried. Money and valuable personal possessions were placed into an envelope marked with a prisoner's name, address, and date of birth, so that they could be returned upon his release. Items that the SS clerk considered worthless, such as rosaries, were reportedly tossed into the moat or, in the case of loose change, probably shared by the guards.

Next, Neumann's head would have been shorn of hair by another prisoner; beards were also shaved. Although prisoners were told that this was done for hygienic reasons, the shaving

Herszel Frydman as a younger man.

also made a prisoner much more noticeable in case he ever tried to escape. It was also clearly a humiliation, an assault on the person—something most had never experienced before.

Afterward, Israel Neumann would have been sent to a storeroom, where he was told to undress completely and hand his clothes to a clerk, who would have placed them in a cloth bag. When—if—he was ever released from Breendonk, they would be returned to him as well.

In this room, he would have met Herszel Frydman, a tailor originally from Poland who was also a prisoner. Among the men sent to Breendonk on September 21, 1940—its second day

The main barracks hallway.

of existence as an *Auffanglager*—Frydman had been arrested along with his three sons, Joseph, Jacques, and David. When the Germans entered Belgium, Frydman and his family, like an estimated one and a half to two million Belgian residents, had fled south to France, hoping to escape.

When German troops continued into France, the Frydmans and most of the others in the exodus realized the futility of remaining there and returned to Belgium. The military administration permitted the reentry of almost anyone who had left the country. But when the Frydmans tried to return to Brussels, where they had a tailor shop and clothing store, Herzel and his sons were arrested, since the *Militärverwaltung* prohibited the return of Jews.

———

Soon after he was incarcerated at Breendonk, fifty-five-year-old Herszel Frydman boldly told Commandant Schmitt that a hernia prevented him from performing the required labor at the camp. When Schmitt asked him what job he could do instead, Frydman told him, "I'm a tailor. What you're wearing, I know how to make it."

Schmitt quickly realized that Frydman's skills might be useful, so he established a tailoring workshop where Frydman could prepare the old Belgian army uniforms that had been stored in the fort as the attire for new prisoners. But Schmitt had another motive in creating the workshop. As a man who took great pride in his appearance, he could not resist the thought of having his own private tailor at Breendonk. So he ordered Frydman to make suits for him and other SS officers. As more prisoners arrived, Frydman convinced Schmitt to allow his three sons to join him in the tailor workshop, saving them from the forced labor outside.

————

That October day, Herszel Frydman altered Israel Neumann's uniform, shortening the trousers and sleeves, since it was intended for a much larger man. Even so, the finished uniform was still too large. Next, he sewed Neumann's prisoner number and a yellow ribbon on the front left pocket and another yellow ribbon on the back of his uniform. The yellow ribbon would identify him as a Jew (a white ribbon designated an "Aryan," the pseudoscientific term the Nazis used to describe what they considered to be a master race of pureblood Germans).

Finally, Israel Neumann—*Häftlingsnummer zweiundzwanzig,* or prisoner number 22—would have been made to run to his new quarters: Room 1, which was more like a concrete cave than a room. Like all the original twelve barracks, it was almost forty feet long and eighteen feet wide, with thick concrete walls and an arched ceiling. Each barrack had two windows darkened by paint at one end and a heavy wooden door—locked from the outside by the guards—at the other. Crammed inside were sixteen bunk beds, stacked two high, eight on each side of a narrow center aisle. As the number of prisoners grew beyond thirty-two, a third bunk would be placed on top of each, so that the room would hold forty-eight men. Near the windows were a small stove, a few tables and stools, and some shelves. Even in summer, the concrete room would be so damp that water would drip regularly from the ceiling.

Once Neumann was inside Room 1, the *Zugführer*—the room leader, who was also a prisoner—might have pointed out his bunk and informed him of the rules and the daily routine.

Or another prisoner might have whispered a few words of instruction.

Or he might have been left alone to figure out the workings of the room and the camp himself.

No matter how he was introduced to Room 1, he would soon meet the other prisoners and discover what Breendonk, and the SS, had in store for him.

4.

THE FIRST PRISONERS
OF ROOM 1

A typical barrack room at Breendonk.

In the weeks before Israel Neumann arrived at Breendonk, only about twenty other prisoners had been sent there. By the end of December, some sixty-five prisoners had been registered. The exact number of prisoners and their dates of arrival and release are not all known, however, since some of the records were lost or destroyed near the end of the German occupation. This was a slow start for a camp that would, for a short time, eventually house as many as 660 prisoners.

During the first ten months, about two-thirds of the prisoners at Breendonk were Jews, almost all of whom had emigrated from other European countries to Belgium. Most were arrested simply because they were Jewish or because they were common criminals already incarcerated when the Germans invaded.

All the early prisoners were initially placed together in Room 1, but as more arrived Schmitt and Prauss made a change. Since every prisoner was classified as either Jew or Aryan, Schmitt decided to split up the two groups and place them in separate barracks that first December. Jewish prisoners remained in Room 1; non-Jews were transferred to Room 6.

Even prisoner numbers reflected the classification system. Before the two groups of prisoners were divided, all incoming prisoners seem to have been given sequential numbers starting with 1. After the prisoners were separated, the numbering system was reconfigured: with few exceptions, Jews were given numbers from 1 to 160, while non-Jews were reallocated numbers over 160. Their original numbers were then reassigned to incoming Jews.

If there was any doubt whether a prisoner was Jewish, Schmitt or Prauss would ask the prisoner on arrival. It didn't matter if the prisoner had been baptized in or had converted to another faith; if he had Jewish parents or grandparents, he was assigned to Room 1.

By the end of December 1940, Room 1 was filling up.

Israel Steinberg, prisoner number 26, was most likely taken to Breendonk the same day as Israel Neumann. Born in Poland and a tailor by trade, he was a petty thief who had been arrested and convicted for pickpocketing in Austria in 1930, with subsequent arrests for the same crime in Germany and Belgium. After he was expelled from Belgium in 1937, he

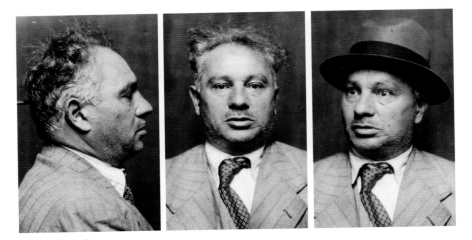

Israel Steinberg.

returned home to Poland, where he claimed to have a wife and five children. In 1938, he tried to make his way to Palestine. On the way, he was arrested in Vienna, expelled from Italy, and ended up in Belgium once again, where he was arrested in July 1939. Police officers had observed him watching people withdraw cash from the bank in a Brussels post office, as if he were planning to rob them. When he was taken into custody, the police found that he did not have a passport, only a Polish identity card. Although he claimed to have arrived in the country seven days earlier, he could not provide officers with an address. Escorted to within a few miles of the border, he was told to cross into Germany and not return. Instead, he traveled to another Belgium town, where he was again caught in the act of robbery. This time, he was sentenced to ten months in jail and placed in the Saint-Gilles Prison in Brussels. After the Nazis took control, they transferred him to Breendonk, where he was told to take care of the pigs, a job that was intended to humiliate him as a Jew.

He came to be called "the pig-man."

———

Ludwig Juliusberger was taken to Breendonk on November 11.

Born in Berlin, he informed the other prisoners in Room 1 that he had studied law and worked as a journalist publishing anti-Nazi pamphlets before fleeing to Austria and then France. He also told them that once he arrived in Belgium, a

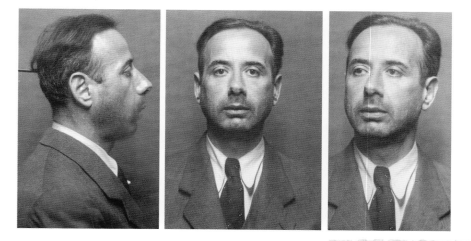

Ludwig Juliusberger.

background check by immigration officials revealed that he had fought in the German army during World War I. Because Belgian authorities suspected him of being pro-Nazi, he, like many other native Germans living in Belgium, was arrested and placed in prison.

Of course, an inmate could tell other prisoners anything; the truth of any story could not be verified. Although

Juliusberger claimed to be a journalist, his police records suggested another story. When Belgian authorities checked his background in Germany, they discovered that before 1932 he had been charged twelve times for forgery, fraud, gambling, and embezzlement. On September 1, 1939, five days after he arrived in Belgium, he was arrested for fraud. He had checked in to a series of Brussels hotels using false names and then left without paying his bill. A Belgian court had sentenced him to fourteen months in jail for fraud—not for being a former soldier in the German army.

By the time his sentence was completed, Belgium was controlled by the German military government, and because Juliusberger was a Jew, Breendonk was his next stop.

He became prisoner number 34.

––––––––––

Paul Lévy.

Paul Lévy, a well-known Belgian radio personality, left Belgium during the eighteen-day invasion, with other employees of his radio station. Warned by his friends not to return because of his Jewish heritage, Lévy ignored their advice. Instead, when he went back to Belgium on July 8, he converted to Catholicism, because of "his beliefs and love for his wife." Soon after, he told German authorities that he would not read the heavily censored and propaganda-filled pro-Nazi news on the radio. After this act of defiance, he was arrested. He arrived at Breendonk on November 29 and was herded down the entrance tunnel to the courtyard, where he was ordered to face the wall.

There, SS-Lieutenant Prauss asked the four prisoners who arrived that day, "Who is a Jew here?"

After the others replied, Lévy, well aware that his recent conversion to Catholicism would not save him, answered, "According to my point of view, no . . . according to yours, surely yes."

Prauss looked at Lévy, shrugged, and then struck him across the face.

When it was his turn to receive his uniform, Lévy was given number 19 and sent outside to work, shoveling dirt into a wheelbarrow. As he attempted to do this, SS-Major Schmitt kicked him three times. Lévy vowed that he would somehow gain his freedom and tell the world about Breendonk.

Lévy believed that his days at the camp would be limited. Unlike the other prisoners, his head had not been shaved the first day. He hoped this was a sign that he was not a long-term prisoner and would be released soon. The next day, however, he was taken from his wheelbarrow and told to run to the courtyard. There, a prisoner waited for him with a razor.

Because Lévy had a thick head of hair, a *Wehrmacht* guard said, "What filth! There must be lice in this forest."

In less than five minutes, Lévy's head was bare, and the reality of a long stay at Breendonk had begun to set in.

Oskar Hoffman.

———

Oskar Hoffman, who arrived on December 5, was assigned to be the first blacksmith at the camp. An Austrian citizen, he and his wife fled to Belgium a few months after the *Anschluss*. When the German invasion began, Hoffman was arrested by

Belgian police for fear that he might be an enemy agent and he was deported to an internment camp in southern France. When he eventually returned to Belgium, an acquaintance from the French camp, perhaps trying to garner favor, informed authorities that Hoffman held anti-Nazi sentiments.

As a result, Hoffman was arrested and sent to Breendonk, where he became prisoner number 17.

Abraham Feldberg, as shown on his 1929 Belgian identity card.

Abraham Feldberg arrived on December 7. Feldberg was a Polish immigrant who had a popular shop in Arlon, a small town in southeast Belgium near the Luxembourg border, where he sold suspenders and other items made from elastic. Sometimes he dressed in a clown costume with a large bowler hat and acted like a buffoon to attract shoppers to his store.

On October 28, the *Militär-verwaltung* enacted a law that required Jewish merchants to display a poster indicating their store was a Jewish business. To comply with this regulation, Feldberg decided to poke fun at it by posting three signs on his front windows. In a report written after the war, an inspector for the town of Arlon noted that not only did Feldberg's large signs irritate the Germans, but his gestures toward the signs also were "not to the Germans' taste."

Not long after, he was arrested and sent to Breendonk, where he became prisoner number 53 and the camp's first shoemaker.

No matter which color ribbon the prisoner was made to wear, the inmates at the fort had a common confusion. They were almost always never told why they had been arrested. They were almost never tried for a crime. They were almost never given a specific sentence to serve.

They were simply locked up and kept in a terrible limbo, waiting for whatever would happen next.

Abraham Feldberg posed in front of his shop in Arlon shortly before his arrest. His shop windows displayed the required announcement that his was a Jewish-owned business.

5.

THE ARTIST OF
ROOM 1

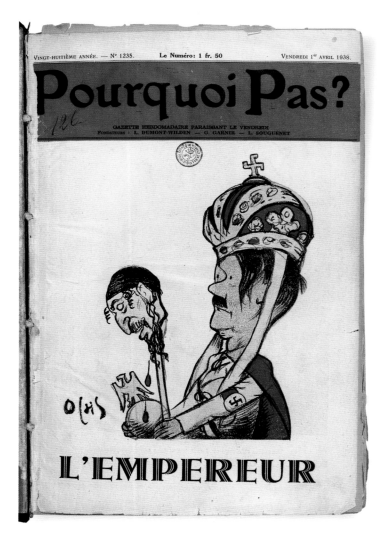

This illustration by Jacques Ochs led to his arrest and incarceration
at Breendonk.

After the war, some of these early prisoners would have been only names in a registration book, especially if they did not survive their imprisonment—except for an unusual turn of events.

Jacques Ochs, an artist who was the director of the Academy of Fine Arts in Liège, Belgium, was arrested on November 17, 1940. His crime was drawing an unflattering image of Adolf Hitler that was published on the cover of the satirical magazine *Pourquoi Pas?*. The illustration was considered anti-Nazi, and someone—rumored to be a Nazi sympathizer who wanted Ochs's job—reported him to German authorities.

After three weeks in solitary confinement in a Liège prison, Ochs was told by a guard that he was going to be freed. Instead, he was placed on a truck and driven to Breendonk. Although Ochs said that he did not consider himself to be a Jew, the SS did, because at least one of his grandparents had been Jewish.

He was sent to Room 1, as prisoner number 56, where he met Israel Neumann and the others.

———

Like Herszel Frydman, Ochs was older and had a disability—in his case from an aviation accident sustained during World War I. Like Frydman, he was fortunate to have been assigned an easier work detail—in Ochs's case, he worked as an assistant in the blacksmith shop.

One day, SS-Major Schmitt called Ochs to his office.

Nummer 56 meldet sich zur Stelle! Ochs told Schmitt and Lieutenant Prauss, who was standing nearby. "Number 56 reporting for duty!"

Sie sind Kunstmaler; machen Sie gleich das Bild vom Herrn Major, Prauss said. "You're a painter; make a portrait of the major right now."

Ochs was given paper, pencils, an eraser, and a very

difficult human model. Major Schmitt sat silently in a chair while Prauss stood over the artist, watching his every pencil stroke. When he was finished, Prauss took the portrait and asked him to leave. Ochs had no idea what the two SS officers thought or wanted.

The next morning, he found out: he was assigned the special duty of *Zeichnendienst*, the Drawing Service, a "job" created especially for him. He still worked in the blacksmith shop but was allowed to draw portraits of the prisoners during certain hours. All drawings, however, were to become the property of Major Schmitt, who wanted to give them to his family and friends as gifts. Although Ochs complied with Schmitt's order to surrender the drawings that he made, he also circumvented it. He often made a second sketch of the same subject, giving the extra version to Schmitt while hiding the original for himself.

Abraham Feldberg, by Jacques Ochs.

During his imprisonment in Room 1, Ochs drew many prisoners, including Israel Neumann, Abraham Feldberg, Israel Steinberg, and Oskar Hoffman. In a book he wrote after the war about his experiences at the camp, Ochs explained that when he asked a prisoner to pose for a portrait, he tried to extend the session as long as possible to allow the man to rest from his heavy labor. In return, he did not mind accepting a crust of the man's bread as a kind of payment. Prisoners were grateful to Ochs

Israel Steinberg, by Jacques Ochs.   *Oskar Hoffman, by Jacques Ochs.*

for drawing them. Since there were no mirrors in the camp, the portraits were their only way to see what they looked like.

One day, a new prisoner was ushered into Ochs's room: a Jew from Antwerp named Alter Bréziner. Ochs was told to draw Bréziner, who was a *schochet,* a man who performed the ritual slaughter of animals for Jews so that the meat would be kosher. Because he had not yet been registered, he was wearing his regular clothes and his hair had not been shaved.

When Ochs had completed his drawing, Bréziner was taken from the room to be processed as a new prisoner. He was issued a number, a classification, and a uniform; then

Alter Bréziner.

45

his beard and head were shaved even though he was an Orthodox Jew. A half hour later, Bréziner—who had become prisoner number 75—was taken back to Ochs for an "after" portrait, the only time Schmitt ever made such a demand. That he chose an Orthodox Jew for such humiliating treatment suggests a racial motive.

For some prisoners, such as Bréziner, Ochs's portraits would be the last, unexpected glimpses of their life.

Alter Bréziner,
by Jacques Ochs.

6

Watching the Prisoners

A Wehrmacht *soldier guards the worksite at Breendonk in June 1941.*
(Kropf photo 28)

Although the daily running of the camp fell to SS-Lieutenant Prauss, he relied on others to help maintain order.

Basic supervision during the first year was provided by *Wehrmacht* soldiers, about forty men who were rotated every three or four months from an army battalion stationed in the nearby city of Mechelen. These soldiers were the sentries who guarded the fort and prevented prisoners from escaping. During the first year, they also escorted new arrivals into the fort, patrolled the hallways, and marched prisoners to the toilets or to the courtyard for *Appell,* or roll call.

Wehrmacht soldiers also monitored prisoners placed in solitary-confinement cells. These cells were, at first, on the left side of the entrance tunnel. There were originally three of them, intended to house disobedient Belgian soldiers when the fort was first built. The SS, however, divided them into six smaller cells, where they placed prisoners who had disobeyed an order, who had arranged to mail a secret letter to someone outside the fort, or who had exhibited poor work performance.

Windowless and unheated, the dark solitary-confinement cells were meant to be oppressive. They had only a wooden bench for sleeping and a small slop bucket (referred to as a "jam jar") for a toilet. Prisoners who received a more severe punishment also had to stand in their cell or in the hallway for long periods of time without moving or even leaning against the wall.

———

Perhaps the people that Prauss counted on most were the *Zugführers*. Prisoners themselves, they served as intermediaries between the camp administration and the inmates. Their primary job was to maintain discipline in the barracks and make certain that all orders were carried out. This often meant that room leaders had to act more like SS guards to accomplish their goals. If they beat a prisoner, no questions were asked by the camp administration.

The *Zugführers* were carefully chosen—not only to create order but, in a way, to create trouble. In the barrack, they were required to dole out the food. Some played favorites, giving more to prisoners they liked. Perhaps that also explained why of the *Zugführers* selected by the end of the first few months to lead the four barracks in use, three of the four were Jews. The idea of a Jewish *Zugführer* upset some of the non-Jewish prisoners, who resented taking orders from him, while Jewish prisoners resented him acting like a Nazi.

These four men may have been singled out initially because they were all born in Germany and spoke the language fluently. All had immigrated to Belgium before the war, and upon the invasion of the German army all were expelled from the country and deported to the French internment camp of Saint-Cyprien because Belgian authorities incorrectly suspected that they were German sympathizers. When they returned to Belgium during the first few months of the occupation, however, all were arrested and sent to Breendonk.

Zugführer *Willi Giersch*.

The men did not know each other before coming to the camp, but they had much in common, especially the desire to save themselves, no matter what the cost.

Zugführer *Sally Lewin.*

Zugführer *Leo Schmandt.*

Willy Giersch, the only non-Jew of the original *Zugführers,* was an early member of the resistance who was arrested for treason and sent to Breendonk in October 1940. Presented with the opportunity to become the first *Zugführer* of Room 1 and soon after the first *Oberarbeitsführer,* the main supervisor of the work site, he gladly agreed. As *Zugführer,* he earned a reputation for beating inmates, especially Jews. A native of Berlin, Giersch did not like the Nazis or their ideology, but he shared their hatred of the Jews and demonstrated this in his brutal behavior toward them.

When Jews and non-Jews were placed into separate barracks in December, he moved with the non-Jews to Room 6, where he continued to assault prisoners. After he learned that the prisoner Joseph Couvreur had stolen cigarette butts from ashtrays in the guard room, he punched him in the mouth so hard that he knocked out three teeth. Smoking by prison-

Sally Lewin, by Jacques Ochs.

ers was strictly prohibited at Breendonk, except on Sunday during the first few months, when the prisoners who worked best were rewarded with one cigarette. However, the smoking prohibition, like many of the camp's rules, was not always enforced across the board. When the tailor Herszel Frydman told Commandant Schmitt that he would be able to perform his work better if he could smoke, Schmitt told him, "I will bring you some cigarettes, but you can't say anything to anyone."

Giersch was released for unspecified reasons in February 1941, after a brief stay in the camp.

———

Sally Lewin and Leo Schmandt were two of the three original Jewish *Zugführers*, part of an unspoken SS plan to turn a victim into an abuser. Like many of the room leaders, they received certain privileges for their cooperation. Lewin, for example, was allowed to have visits from his wife, and his son was permitted to take a vacation of several weeks in Germany during the war. Schmandt was freed by the Germans in 1942, under the condition that he divorce his Christian wife, since marriages between Jews and non-Jews were not permitted by the Nazis. When he divorced her, he was released from Breendonk and spent the rest of the occupation fearing that he would be deported to Germany.

———————

But the most brutal of the initial *Zugführers* was in charge of Room 1 at the end of 1940.

His name was Walter Obler.

7

THE *ZUGFÜHRER* OF ROOM 1

Oberarbeitsführer *Walter Obler, standing on the hill, supervises prisoners at the work site on June 13, 1941. (Kropf photo 1)*

Israel Neumann and other prisoners of Room 1 would have been well acquainted with Walter Obler. In fact, almost every prisoner knew him, because after Willy Giersch was released from the camp, Obler replaced him as the *Oberarbeitsführer*. He had the enviable position of both assigning jobs to prisoners and being the head supervisor of their forced labor; his daily decisions could save a prisoner's life or bring about his death.

A Berlin-born Jew, Obler moved to Vienna, Austria, with his family when he was fourteen. There, he was arrested twice, once for theft and another time for fraud, and spent almost four months in jail for the two offenses. After the German-Austrian *Anschluss* in 1938, he escaped to Belgium without obtaining the proper immigration papers. His non-Jewish wife, Maria Skamene, followed him shortly.

Walter Obler, 1938.

After Obler returned from the French internment camp during the summer of 1940, the SIPO-SD arrested him and prepared to send him to Breendonk. When they discovered that he was married to a non-Jew, they punished him by castrating his left testicle, according to testimony he gave at a trial after the war. Then they warned him that they might remove the other if he did not serve the Nazis well at Breendonk. Some have doubted his explanation, believing that his castration might have occurred for medical reasons and that Obler invented the story for sympathy. Nonetheless, for his good behavior at Breendonk, his wife was frequently allowed to visit him at the camp.

As *Zugführer*, Obler quickly developed a reputation for extreme cruelty, as well as for his allegiance to SS-Lieutenant Prauss. If a guard or an SS officer punished a prisoner, Obler often administered an additional penalty to the same man afterward. Once, Obler discovered the prisoner Hertz Jospa sharing his soup with a sick and starving prisoner. Obler struck Jospa, then said, "Oh . . . you have a good heart. I warn you, I warn you, you must not have a good heart here." If he found prisoners with extra food, such as a carrot or a cabbage, stolen out of hunger, he beat them.

He wanted to make certain that the barracks he supervised would be a model for the others. Perhaps he thought it would save his life if he collaborated with the Nazis and became an ideal inmate himself. As one prisoner later put it, Obler was a Jew "who considered it preferable to join the side of the wolves than remain with the sheep."

Paul Lévy remembered what Obler told him the first day he walked into Room 1: "Here you . . . speak only German. You obey all orders. . . . Obey and work, otherwise watch out! And don't forget . . . the major is the boss of the lieutenant, the lieutenant is my boss, and I am your boss. Obey!"

Although Obler was never reported to have beaten Lévy, he had no difficulty stealing food from packages sent to Lévy by his wife. During the first eight months or so, prisoners were allowed to receive one package of food about every two weeks to supplement their meager daily ration of food. The contents, however, could be pilfered by the guards long before they reached the intended recipient. Sometimes a prisoner would open his rifled package to find only some clothing and the scent of the stolen food still clinging to the fabric. Once, when Obler helped himself to a can of sardines from Paul Lévy's package, he opened the can and spread the sardines on a piece of bread. Lévy could do nothing about the blatant theft except watch Obler eat.

Another day, a team of prisoners working outside came upon some civilian workers. Usually prisoners were suspicious

The work site was essentially the entire outdoor area of the fort, where prisoners were forced to remove the tons of sand covering it. (Kropf photo 26)

of any outside laborers for fear that they were Nazi sympathizers. This day, however, the workers seemed trustworthy, especially when they promised to leave two sandwiches for the emaciated prisoners in a special hiding place. At the appointed time, one of the prisoners retrieved the sandwiches and concealed them in the pockets of his uniform.

But someone had spotted the crime, and soon the prisoner was called to the camp office, where the sandwiches were taken from him and he was beaten. SS-Lieutenant Prauss demanded to know where the sandwiches had come from, but the prisoner refused to say. Even the civilian workers were brought in and asked whether part of their lunch had disappeared. None of them acknowledged any missing food. Prauss was furious and struck the prisoner again, then sent him away for additional punishment.

Zugführer *Walter Obler beating a prisoner, by Jacques Ochs.*

Not long after, however, some prisoners saw Obler shamelessly eating the sandwiches that the prisoner had taken from the hiding place. Obler, they realized, had been the informant.

As for the prisoner who had been caught, Prauss made him stand with his nose to the courtyard wall until six o'clock that night, burdened with a heavy backpack of stones, a commonplace punishment at Breendonk. He was then put in solitary confinement for a time, with only water and half his usual food.

It was no wonder that the prisoners feared Obler. Like Prauss, he seemed to be everywhere and know everything.

Walter Obler and his wife, Maria Skamene, 1939.

Not surprisingly, Obler could also be influenced by the other prisoners—for the right price. If a prisoner had access to money or jewelry, Obler would often strike a bargain with him. As the *Oberarbeitsführer,* he wielded the ultimate power, which he did not hesitate to use to his advantage. For a certain payment, Obler would promise to give a prisoner a less demanding job on the work site. The jewelry and money he accumulated for these favors were hidden under the roof tiles of the pigsty, by his reported accomplice Israel Steinberg. Every now and then, when Obler's wife came to visit, he would slip her the money and jewelry he had collected. One day, his hiding place was found by the SS, and Obler and Steinberg were punished for a time. Many prisoners did not believe that Steinberg was guilty of helping Obler, though. Even if he had, he was hardly in a position to deny the *Zugführer* anything.

8

A DAY AT
BREENDONK

A barrack room.

During the fall of 1940, a typical day for the prisoners of Breendonk began at six a.m., when they were awakened by a guard screaming, *Aufstehen!* "Get up!" Prisoners were expected to pull on their pants and shoes and go into the long corridor outside their barrack room, where there was a row of cold-water faucets. They had a few moments to wash their upper bodies and faces, often without soap. They dried themselves off with a small scrap of dirty towel.

Prisoners had only a few moments to wash their upper bodies with cold water from the taps in the hallway.

Then came the next command: *Austreten!* "Go out!"

The prisoners lined up in rows of two before running to the toilets, which were outside. In each of the two courtyards, a small brick building contained four "toilets"; that is, four narrow cubicles without doors, each with a hole in the floor. A communal urinal was outside the toilet block. The toilets and the urinals had no flushing mechanism; all waste simply fell into a cesspool beneath. Prisoners were not allowed to use any paper, either. One barrack of up to forty-eight prisoners had only ten minutes to use the eight toilets.

All the time, they were watched by guards training rifles at them and yelling, *Schnell, schnell!* "Hurry, hurry!"

Afterward, the prisoners returned to the corridor outside their room and waited as a few prisoners cleaned it. These prisoners had to empty the two buckets that served as toilets during the night; often these were overflowing. Then they had to clean up any spills and sweep the room before the prisoners could go back inside.

Bed making, or Bettenbau, *was a required daily chore, and failure to do it properly often resulted in punishment.*

When the room was ready, the prisoners prepared themselves for the daily ritual of *Bettenbau,* or bed making. As if they were soldiers, they had to make their beds according to rules established by SS-Lieutenant Prauss. Each inmate was required to transform "his bed, a shapeless cloth bag filled with straw, into a cuboid with sharp, crisp edges." To accomplish this, he had to try to spread the straw out in the mattress sack as flat as possible, into every one of the four corners. Then he covered the mattress with a blanket and raked it with a piece of wood to make it level. All the mattresses in the same row of beds were to be perfectly level with each other. Like every thing else at Breendonk, *Bettenbau* had to be completed rapidly, in no more than seven minutes. With only two feet between each row of bunk beds and forty-eight prisoners per barrack, this proved to be a daunting task.

Next was the inspection of prisoners. The men had to

A day's meals at Breendonk: acorn coffee, a watery soup of vegetable scraps for lunch, and bread.

make sure that their uniforms were properly buttoned and that their pants hung over their boots. Anyone who failed the inspection was deprived of breakfast that day.

At seven a.m., two prisoners assigned to the chore of *Essenholen,* or food server, went to the camp kitchen, where they were required to stand at attention and announce their room number before they could retrieve breakfast for their room.

Roll call, or Appell, *required prisoners to line up in the courtyard four times a day. At the right end of the above rows are three early prisoners: Israel Steinberg (back row), Israel Neumann (middle row), and Oskar Hoffman (front row). (Kropf photo 10)*

Breakfast consisted of bread and two cups of "coffee" made from acorns stewed in hot water. The bread was limited to three and one-half ounces per prisoner (the equivalent of two and one half slices of today's typical sandwich bread).

In the barracks, the *Zugführer* gave the prisoners a slice of bread and ladled the coffee into an enamel bowl. Prisoners savored each morsel of bread with the bitter drink and often moistened their fingers to pick up the crumbs from the table so that nothing remained uneaten.

At seven thirty a.m., it was time to perform twenty minutes of calisthenics in the courtyard, followed by *Appell* and military drill. *Appell* was as precise as *Bettenbau*. Prisoners were required to line up in rows of three, arranged by barrack and by height, and stand at attention without moving. Jews stood on the left, non-Jews on the right. Each *Zugführer* reported the number of prisoners in his barrack to the SS officer in charge. All the while, as the prisoners stood there, they had a clear view of the stables where the commandant's horses were kept, the stalls labeled with the horses' names, a consideration not granted to the prisoners themselves.

When roll call was finished, the prisoners were ordered to attention as SS-Lieutenant Prauss walked into the courtyard. Then a lower-ranking SS officer put them through a military drill as if they were soldiers in front of their commanding officer: *Augen rechts! Augen geradeaus!* "Look right! Look straight ahead!"

Next the most dreaded word of all was called: *Arbeiten!* "Work!"

———

The labor that most of the prisoners were forced to do was overwhelming and completely meaningless. They had to remove more than 500,000 tons of sand—a true mountain— that had both camouflaged and protected the fort since 1914. Except for the gatehouse and the north wall of the barracks wing, the fort had been buried in sand scooped up during the excavation of the moat. Now the SS wanted the sand removed and instead used in the construction of an earthen wall around the outer edge of the moat in order to screen the camp from passersby on the nearby Brussels-Antwerp highway.

At the work site, the inmates were assigned their jobs. Prisoners could be told to shovel (filling or emptying wheelbarrows or large metal carts with sand) or drive a wooden

One of the jobs assigned by Oberarbeitsführer *Obler was pushing or pulling a wheelbarrow filled with sand or rocks. (Kropf photo 3)*

wheelbarrow (shuttling between the sand pile and the carts where they were emptied). The strongest prisoners were the cart movers, who, working in teams of four, maneuvered the carts on portable rails to the other side of the moat, where the sand was dumped. Cart movers had to make about twenty-five round trips a day, which was not easy, considering that the cart's turning mechanism was often uncooperative. Obler, Prauss, and the guards monitored the prisoners carefully, ready to mete out physical punishment to anyone who moved too slowly. Some guards even tried to wreak havoc on the prisoners by causing mishaps with the wheelbarrows or carts.

It was backbreaking work, fraught with danger. It was also, one former prisoner said, "heavy work for starving men.

But that was SS policy, designed to weaken us, to tame us, to make us admit defeat."

Prisoners had to work all year in all types of weather. During one rainstorm, the guards were sheltered under a tarpaulin that SS-Lieutenant Prauss had rigged for them, but the prisoners were drenched as they waded through mud and shoveled the heavy, waterlogged sand. By the time they were allowed to stop—just after the storm had passed—they were sent to their barracks completely soaked. Even though it was relatively warm outside, the concrete rooms were damp and chilly. The only place to warm up was by the one stove in

Injuries on the worksite were not uncommon, but there was no sickbay at Breendonk until February 1941. (Kropf photo 23)

each barrack, except that there was rarely any fuel. Prisoners were usually not allowed to have any wood, though they would often secretly bring some in from the work site or other places around the camp. If the wood was discovered, it was confiscated and the prisoners in that barrack were deprived of food for a day.

Many prisoners tried their best to make life at Breendonk survivable. Some, like Herszel Frydman and Jacques Ochs, appealed to SS-Major Schmitt so that they could avoid the heavy labor required of most inmates. Others were given different duties, such as Israel Steinberg, the swineherd, or Oskar Hoffman, the blacksmith. Still others treated the work site as a competition and tried to keep motivated. But for many, the work detail was more than they could bear, especially when coupled with the meager rations.

––––––––

The workday during the first few months was grueling enough. Prisoners worked two four-hour sessions with a lunch break between. Lunch consisted of two bowls of thin soup that contained some beans, onions, and potatoes, as well as a scrap or two of ground meat. The trick for some prisoners, if the

Three prisoners in front of the stove, by Jacques Ochs.

Zugführer allowed it, was to linger and wait until most of the other men in the barrack were served, so that they could receive a ladle from the bottom of the soup pot, where the more solid contents collected and the broth thickened.

After the second work session, prisoners had to clean their tools, brush off their clothing, and thoroughly scrub any mud from their boots before entering the barracks. They were allowed to wash their hands before another *Appell* was taken in their room. Finally, dinner was brought to them by the *Essenholen:* a little more than four ounces of bread and two more cups of acorn coffee. On rare occasions, a tablespoon of margarine or jam was included with the meal. In the early months, prisoners were given a few bits of meat and a boiled potato on Sundays.

Another roll call was followed by a second planned trip to the toilets. One more roll call was done, and then at eight p.m. it was time for bed. Prisoners had to remove their socks and place them in their boots, lined up precisely with the toes pointing toward the center aisle at the foot of their bunks. They had just five minutes to prepare before the guard made a final check of the room and turned off the solitary bulb that lit the room.

———————

Nights at Breendonk, according to Jacques Ochs, found the prisoners "lying on their cot . . . where water trickles down the walls. They are waiting for sleep to forget their untold suffering—their bodies are sore, their limbs bruised, hunger tortures them. And the night is long, feverish and hallucinatory in this heavy atmosphere . . . , where the odors of unwashed bodies, sweat, wet clothes, and ammonia mingle . . . the complaints, muffled and pathetic; the snoring; the stifled sobs; the curses. . . . These are the nights of Breendonk!"

Prisoners may have been hungry, but there was more

A work by Jacques Ochs, entitled Jewish Section. *Researchers have debated whether certain drawings that he did at Breendonk reflected Ochs's own anti-Semitism.*

food than there would be eventually. For Christmas 1940, prisoners were even allowed to take a collection of money, often hidden in the packages they received from home, for some Christmas treats: cold cuts, fresh fruit, and even chocolate candy. SS-Major Schmitt himself went to Brussels to purchase the goods, and the prisoners, Jews and non-Jews alike, had a Christmas Eve celebration in their barracks. Later that same night, the *Wehrmacht* soldiers celebrated in the Breendonk canteen. Drunk and rowdy, they began firing their guns down the corridors.

For these first prisoners, life at Breendonk was terrible but still manageable. As Paul Lévy recalled, "All this seemed absolutely incredible for anyone who knew what happened at Breendonk later."

As the new year began, everything would change for the worse.

THE FIRST DEATHS

January–June 1941

9.

CHANGES

A guard tower at Breendonk.

At the beginning of 1941, the prisoners' food ration was reduced. The little meat that had sometimes been placed into the daily soup disappeared almost completely. The meat served on Sundays was also eliminated, as was the Sunday cigarette for prisoners who had been singled out for working hard.

This mirrored changes in food supplies throughout Belgium. Military officials had claimed that the "civilian population will never know hunger"; by January 1941, however, the *Militärverwaltung* had difficulty supplying enough bread, butter, potatoes, and other staples to the general population. As a result, many Belgians turned to the black market, but there was no black market at Breendonk, only the occasional packages that some families sent to their incarcerated loved ones. Since these were often opened and the contents stolen by the SS, the prisoners began to suffer.

Another change occurred in February, not long after a small group of new prisoners arrived. Among them were Ernest Landau and Julius Nathan.

Landau, a journalist, had escaped from his Austrian homeland after *Kristallnacht* and made his way to Brussels, where after the start of the German occupation, he began to work for the fledgling resistance movement. His job was to translate French leaflets into German; these would then be left where *Wehrmacht* soldiers would find them in the hope that they would learn the truth about Hitler. One day the SIPO-SD located the shop that printed the German leaflets; they also discovered Landau's handwritten corrections on the documents. When one of the

Ernest Landau.

print shop workers mentioned Landau's name during an interrogation, Landau was tracked down, arrested, and forced to give a writing sample. After his handwriting was matched to the corrections, his interrogation began.

For three days and nights without stop, Landau was questioned and beaten at the SIPO-SD headquarters on Avenue Louise in Brussels. His interrogators hit him with steel rods, burned his face and lips with cigarettes, and broke his glasses. By the end of his ordeal, his face was so swollen that he could not even take a sip of water. Two weeks after his arrest, he was taken to Breendonk. When he entered Room 1, the other prisoners were stunned by his appearance.

Like all Breendonk prisoners, he had been assigned a number (31) and a category (Jew), but Landau had received

Julius Nathan, 1938.

a more detailed classification. Although most of the Jews at Breendonk were arrested only for "racial reasons" and wore a plain yellow ribbon, a red ribbon had been sewn above the yellow ribbon on Landau's jacket; this designated him as a political prisoner. Landau had the same dual classification as Paul Lévy, which made both men more vulnerable at the camp. Because political prisoners were seen as threats by the guards, they could be targeted for almost any infraction. As Lévy explained, political prisoners had "to be submissive. To seem to obey, to play along with the farce of discipline. To respect the stupid rules of camp life. But to keep one's dignity (without saying it too loudly)."

Julius Nathan, a textile salesman, was in even more trouble from the start—not because he was beaten, but because the sixty-one-year-old man suffered from asthma.

During his first night at Breendonk, he was unable to

sleep. Every time he lay down, he choked so hard that he could not breathe. The next morning, he looked exhausted, but *Oberarbeitsführer* Obler sent him to the work site with most of the other prisoners. Although his age and his asthma made it difficult for him to push the wheelbarrow that he was assigned, Obler and SS-Lieutenant Prauss watched him closely, even following him, to make sure that he didn't stop to rest for a moment. Finally, after two weeks of strenuous labor, he dropped his wheelbarrow one day and collapsed on the ground. He was out of breath, exhausted, and unable to move.

The other prisoners at the work site pleaded with him to stand up. They did not want him to make his situation any worse. They were worried that if Obler and Prauss thought he was pretending to be unable to work, this would provoke their anger.

No matter what they said, Nathan wouldn't move. When Obler arrived, he pulled Nathan up by the collar and dragged him inside, down the long barracks corridor. There was no medical care at that point at Breendonk, and no one would consider taking Nathan to a hospital. Besides, Prauss had been heard to say, *Für mich, um krank zu sein, muss man sich melden mit dem Kopf unter dem Arm.* "For me, being sick means that you must report with your head under your arm." In other words, the prisoner had to be practically dead to be considered sick.

In the minds of Obler and Prauss, the only place for him was solitary confinement. So Nathan was beaten and placed in one of the small, dark solitary cells. His death—the first at Breendonk—took place a few hours later, out of the sight of the other prisoners, on February 17, 1941.

———

The news shocked most prisoners. Until that day, no matter how terrible the conditions at the camp were, they had managed to survive, despite the deprivations, hard labor, and abuse. The possibility of death had seemed to lurk only in its shadows.

Now that possibility had become all too plausible. There would be many more deaths to follow.

10

THE FIRST ESCAPE

The door to one of the Revier *rooms.*

The only reaction Commandant Schmitt had to Nathan's death was fury—not that a man had died, but that news of his death had traveled to Londerzeel, a village six miles from the camp, by five thirty that same afternoon. Schmitt suspected that a *Wehrmacht* soldier had mentioned it to someone, so he quickly forbade his staff from reporting any news from the fort to outsiders.

Nathan's death may have had two other consequences.

————

Five days later, a *Revier,* or sickbay, was mentioned for the first time in the camp logbook. Two adjacent rooms—one for non-Jews and one for Jews—were set aside at the end of the barracks corridor.

Dr. Adolph Singer, by Jacques Ochs.

Waiting to be admitted to the Revier, *by Jacques Ochs.*

A Jewish prisoner who had been a doctor in Vienna, Adolph Singer, was assigned to work in the *Revier* and to make "house calls" in the barracks on Sundays. On his rounds, he carried with him a cigar box that contained his limited supply of medicine: aspirin, if a prisoner had the flu, and iodine, Vaseline, and bandages if he had serious cuts or scrapes from working outdoors. Dr. Hans Köchling, a German military doctor, visited the *Revier* infrequently, never more than once or twice a week and usually much less often.

Sacha Frenkel, by Jacques Ochs.

But receiving even this rudimentary medical care was difficult. Prisoners had to report to the *Revier* early in the morning, where SS-Lieutenant Prauss usually waited for them. He would interrogate and often beat them, then send them to work anyway. As a result, very few prisoners were allowed to enter the *Revier* under Prauss's watch.

This may have been the case when, in early April, forty-three-year-old Sacha Frenkel, who had been at Breendonk about six months, showed signs of pneumonia. He had already been beaten by *Zugführer* Lewin so often that he had festering sores on his head; Lewin seemed to take pleasure in repeatedly battering

Sacha Frenkel.

him about the face, trying to hit his previous wounds. But on the day that he developed pneumonia, Prauss refused to admit him to the *Revier*. The next day, when Frenkel was too weak to get out of bed, Prauss became enraged, took him to the courtyard, and doused him with cold water. He died later that day. On his death certificate, Dr. Köchling indicated that he died of "bronchopneumonia and heart failure." No mention was made of the severe beatings that Lewin had inflicted. This was not surprising, for even when he completed a death certificate, Köchling rarely examined the prisoner's corpse in person and never gave the true cause of death.

Perhaps a second result of Nathan's death occurred two days later, when a prisoner decided to escape.

The daily logbook of the camp noted that on February 19, 1940, a prisoner was found to be missing at the five p.m. *Appell*. No other information was recorded, neither the prisoner's number nor name. It was almost as if the camp administration was so embarrassed by the escape that information about it was withheld. But after the war, details came to light during interviews with Jacques Frydman, one of Herszel Frydman's sons, and Mrs. Verdickt, who lived across the street from the camp.

Frydman recalled that the prisoner who escaped was nicknamed *Le Flitser*, or the Flash. A charming man, he had succeeded in ingratiating himself with the SS and the *Wehrmacht* soldiers so well that he was given the privilege of taking the camp laundry to Mrs. Verdickt's house once or twice a week. The guards paid no attention to him, because he had earned their trust.

One day, the Flash came to the tailor's workshop and asked, "You don't have any street clothes—a jacket, some pants, anything—do you?"

Frydman remembered a sack of clothing he had found that contained everything the Flash might need to camouflage himself as a man on the street. Without hesitation, Frydman gave it to him.

Sometime later, the same man arrived at Mrs. Verdickt's house as usual, carrying the camp laundry. He was etched indelibly in her memory, for on that day he had a swollen face from a terrible beating.

"It was Prauss," he announced, before adding that he planned to escape that day. He told her that he had hidden some clothes in a shed on her property. Then he went to change and fled.

That evening, after the escape was discovered, SS-Major Schmitt and SS-Lieutenant Prauss asked Mrs. Verdickt if she had seen the prisoner. She told them she had, then led them to the shed, where she showed them the prison uniform he had left behind.

By that time, Schmitt and the other SS officers living in her house had been drinking heavily and wanted to shoot Mrs. Verdickt and her husband on the spot. But Schmitt's wife intervened and saved their lives.

From that point, prisoners were no longer allowed to fetch water from or take laundry to Mrs. Verdickt's house without an accompanying guard.

———

Although the camp logbook never revealed the escapee's name, other records mentioned that a prisoner named Herz Nisenholz left the camp in February 1941. The records do not indicate where he was from, why he was arrested, when he entered the camp, or even what his prisoner number was. The records are, in fact, blank . . . except for an entry mentioning that Nisenholz left Breendonk that month.

The question that has puzzled researchers is whether Nisenholz was *Le Flitser*.

Additional information about Nisenholz can be found today in the archives of the immigration police housed in the National Archives of Belgium in Brussels. Born in 1900 in a Polish town (now part of Ukraine), Nisenholz lived the life of a thief from an early age. From 1924 to 1937, he was arrested ten times (five times in Poland, twice in France, and once each in Austria, Switzerland, and Germany) for stealing, pickpocketing, and using false identity papers. Each time he was arrested, he gave a different name or birthplace or even birthday so it would be hard to trace him.

Herz Nisenholz (the spelling of his name as recorded in the Breendonk archives) shown in mug shots: (top) Vienna police photograph, 1935; (bottom) Strasbourg police photograph, 1937.

Then he arrived in Belgium, where he was charged with stealing the wallet of a poultry merchant at a public market in Brussels. He served eight months in prison, but when he had completed his sentence in May 1940, the *Militärverwaltung* was in power and not anxious to release Nisenholz. Six times that spring and summer, he wrote the director of the prison asking about his discharge. Finally, on September 18, 1940, he politely requested that he either be released or transferred to an internment camp, probably thinking that such a camp would be preferable to a prison.

On October 4, his request was granted: he was sent to Breendonk, a type of camp that he most likely had never envisioned. He charmed his way into an easier chore, but something had happened during the two days after Nathan's death, and he had been beaten. On February 19, 1941, it is most likely Nisenholz—*Le Flitser*—who risked his life and escaped, one of only a handful of prisoners to successfully do so.

11.

DESPAIR

An unidentified prisoner, by Jacques Ochs.

Other prisoners may have thought of escape as spring arrived, but the unlikely odds for success would have stopped them. The heavy labor and the lack of food had begun to take their toll.

If a prisoner failed to work adequately on the work site, a guard wrote down his number. At lunch, he would then be deprived of his soup and punished further. Sometimes the offending prisoner was handed a pickax to hold with both hands at arm's length. Then he was ordered to squat and stand up in slow motion over and over again, until his strength began to falter.

A former prisoner described it like this: "As soon as the hands [of the prisoner] weaken and shake, a sentry armed with

A Breendonk prisoner forced to squat and stand up quickly and repeatedly while holding a pickax at shoulder level, by Jacques Ochs.

a switch strikes the fingers of the victim. . . . [A] 23-year-old Jew lost four fingers off the right hand from gangrene that set in as a consequence of this treatment."

————————

Depriving the prisoners of food when their daily ration was already so minimal produced terrible misery.

When the prisoner Willem Pauwels, a Brussels artist who wrote and distributed an anti-Nazi underground newspaper, arrived at the camp on April 2, he was carrying a package of sandwiches wrapped in paper. Standing in the courtyard, waiting to be registered, he noticed a nearby prisoner breaking rocks. The two men exchanged glances, and Pauwels intuited that the man was very hungry. He wanted to give him the sandwiches but realized that if he threw them to the man, they would fall into a pigsty filled with dung.

"Just throw it," the prisoner urged.

Pauwels hesitated a moment, then tossed them to the prisoner. As he predicted, the sandwiches fell out of the paper and landed in the wet manure.

Pauwels later recalled that "the guy jumped on those sandwiches covered in dung and ate them, as they were, in a blink of the eye." He looked away in disgust but admitted, "Fifteen days later, I would have done exactly the same thing."

————————

Ludwig Juliusberger was in such despair over the conditions at Breendonk that one day he spoke out to the other prisoners in Room 1 about the bread they were given to eat: it wasn't good, it wasn't enough to sustain them. After his tirade was reported by another prisoner, he was accused of mutiny and taken outside. There he was forced to dig his grave as SS-Major Schmitt stood over him pointing a gun. He was not shot, but the abuse continued.

On the work site, Juliusberger was watched closely by

Obler and Prauss; his every misstep was punished. He was deprived of food so often by *Zugführer* Obler that at night, as Jacques Ochs recalled, he would sit on his bunk "waiting for the right moment to try to steal from the cupboards where the meager provisions of his fellow prisoners were hidden. . . . More than once he was caught."

On another day, Juliusberger again addressed the prisoners of Room 1 when Obler was absent, reportedly telling them, "The day will come when those SS who rule over you will be defeated. Then, you will be their

Abraham Feldberg and Ludwig Juliusberger, by Jacques Ochs.

accusers and you will have to be able to look at them straight in the face. So do not let them humiliate you. React! Keep your dignity!"

When someone informed him about Juliusberger's brave speech, Obler transferred him to *Zugführer* Lewin's barrack with a "special recommendation" for unrelenting labor and punishments and more deprivation of food. Before long, he had lost so much weight that he looked like a skeleton, except that his extremities were swollen, a sign that he was suffering from starvation edema, an affliction that would soon become all too common at Breendonk. Because of the poor diet, reduced protein levels allowed water to leak out of his blood vessels. This caused the face, stomach, wrists, and ankles to swell.

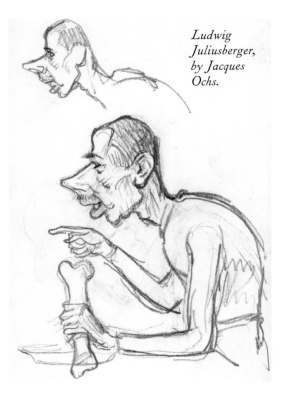

Ludwig Juliusberger, by Jacques Ochs.

Juliusberger would do anything for food; if Prauss told him to act like a monkey, he did just that, to earn the reward of a crust of bread. He agreed one day to do fifteen turns like a ballerina for two loaves of bread. He won his prize, which "he devoured in less than a half hour. That night he soiled his mattress."

Juliusberger could not take the abuse any longer. He had toiled at the work site for a few hours when he suddenly jumped into the shallow water of the moat, hoping to drown. Prauss waded in after him and pulled him out, then slapped his face a few times; suicide was not permissible at Breendonk, although Juliusberger would not be the last to try. He was taken inside and placed in solitary confinement, where even the *Wehrmacht* guards pitied him and gave him crusts of bread.

But it wasn't enough to save him.

He died on April 9, 1941. According to his death certificate, it was a "natural death."

Two months later, another prisoner, a hatmaker named Jacob Kiper, who had spent
five months at Breendonk, snapped. Like all
inmates, he had been unable to write his family
members during his first three months of captivity. After that time, prisoners were then allowed
to send one letter, written only in German,
once a month. Kiper had struggled with this
prohibition. Somehow, he had found a civilian

Jacob Kiper

workman to smuggle letters in and out of Breendonk so that he
could keep in touch with his wife. Kiper also offered the same

SS-Lieutenant Arthur Prauss yelling at a starving prisoner, by Jacques Ochs.

"postal service" to Jacques Ochs, who wished to communicate with his sister.

One day, Kiper's participation in the scheme was discovered. As a result, he was beaten and placed in solitary confinement, where he was forced to stand up until the next morning. When he was allowed to return to Room 1 the next day, he was despondent.

"I cannot remember ever spending a night like that," Kiper told the others. Not long after, he began to talk about killing himself, though other prisoners discouraged such an idea.

A few days later, on June 11, in the middle of his morning work, Kiper had reached his limit. Perhaps he had seen Juliusberger's attempt, perhaps others had told him about it, but Kiper was taking no chances. When the guards weren't looking, he filled his jacket pockets with heavy stones. Then he threw himself into the moat where it was deepest and stayed beneath the water.

By the time he was pulled out a long time later, he was dead.

————

In all, seven prisoners died between February and the end of June. At least six of them were Jewish; the name or number of the seventh victim was never recorded.

12

A PICTURE-PERFECT CAMP

The moat surrounding Breendonk, as captured in an SS photograph taken in the summer of 1941. (Kropf photo 37)

No matter how unbearable the conditions had become for prisoners, Commandant Schmitt believed that his camp was the epitome of a perfectly run *Auffanglager*. To show his SS superiors how splendid a job he was doing at Breendonk, he took the unusual step of arranging for a photographer to take pictures of the inmates going through their daily routine.

The man, Otto Kropf, was a professional photographer in Germany before he was called to duty by the *Wehrmacht*. Trained as a war correspondent, he was assigned to the 612th Propaganda Company, which accompanied German troops during their invasion of Belgium. For the next year and a half, Kropf took many photographs of everyday Belgian life. When he was brought to Breendonk by Schmitt, his instructions were to take photos of "Jews and non-Belgian prisoners." Photos of Belgian citizens, if published, might garner unwanted sympathy from the public.

The resulting images are the only known ones taken at Breendonk during the war. They would have remained lost from history if a Dutch photography collector named Otto Spronk had not heard about a sale of Kropf's Belgian slides and negatives at a German auction house in 1986. He purchased the lot and was surprised to find how well Kropf had documented the German occupation of Belgium. The collection included two rolls of negatives containing photographs of Breendonk. The first, labeled JUDEN - KZ BREENDONCK.13.6.41, or JEWS - BREENDONK CONCENTRATION CAMP, JUNE 13, 1941, held twenty-two photographs. The second, taken on an unspecified later date, had fifteen additional photos.

The photographs attempted to give a sanitized sense of the camp. Well-dressed arriving prisoners faced the wall in the courtyard. Working prisoners loaded and pushed wheelbarrows, removed stones, and filled and transported heavy

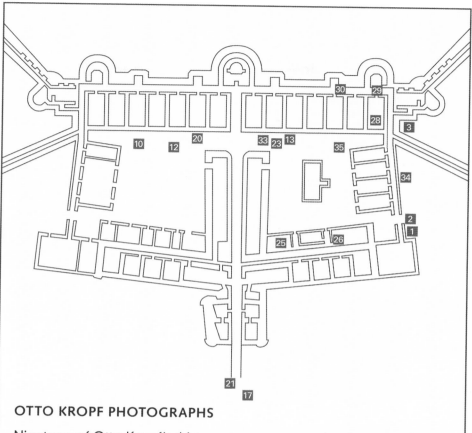

OTTO KROPF PHOTOGRAPHS

Nineteen of Otto Kropf's thirty-seven propaganda photographs have been used throughout this book as illustrations; they can be found on pages 20, 25, 28, 47, 53, 56, 63, 65, 66, 91, 94, 95, 97, 115, 122, 123, 135, and 142. The caption for each photo contains the number of its position on the roll. The map above/below gives the location where each photograph was taken. Numbers 28, 29, and 30 were photographed on the earth-covered roof of the fort.

metal carts on rails. Obedient prisoners awaited their orders at *Appell*. Frolicking companions Schmitt and Lump displayed their affection for each other. Smiling SS officers posed proudly in front of the camp entrance. But a closer look at the photos revealed prisoners who were injured (Kropf photos 2 and 23),

SS-Major Philipp Schmitt playing with his dog, Lump. (Kropf photo 13)

emaciated (photo 29), and suffering the effects of punishment (photos 23 and 33).

What the photos did not reveal were the changed work conditions at the camp. Instead of two four-hour shifts with a lunch break between, the SS administration decided to institute a more rigorous schedule during the summer of 1941: an eight-hour workday, which began at six o'clock and ran without break until two o'clock. Prisoners who broke any rules during that time were sent to the courtyard to face the wall, and deprived of their lunch.

They did not reveal that if work was stopped because of a downpour, SS-Lieutenant Prauss counted the amount of time lost. After lunch, the prisoners were forced to make up the missed work. On other days, though, Prauss might decide that an extra four hours of work was required, so that the men had to labor for twelve straight hours. The work schedule seemed to depend completely upon his whims.

Finally, the photographs also did not reveal the tricks that Prauss used to torture the prisoners mentally. He knew that everyone awaited the sound of the whistle that called them to lunch. From time to time, he would sound the whistle—their only source of time—well before lunch, then order the men back to work. He might repeat the whistle a number of times until the prisoners gave up hope that they would eat lunch that day.

Once, Prauss punished all the prisoners when a packet of tobacco went missing from one of the civilian laborers who worked at the camp and no one would admit the theft; no

Despite the attempt to portray a picture-perfect camp, this photograph by Otto Kropf reveals a prisoner with a facial injury (far right). (Kropf photo 2)

inmate had lunch that day. The prisoner Frans Fischer remembered that punishing everyone "for the crime of an unknown culprit" seemed to fill Prauss's heart with joy.

One afternoon, as the prisoners stood at *Appell* waiting to be released for lunch, Prauss held up a piece of paper and announced that it contained the numbers of twelve men who had disobeyed the camp rule against smoking a discarded cigarette butt. He encouraged the twelve to come forward. Five men took a step toward him and were told to face the wall.

But Prauss was not pleased.

"For the last time, who has been smoking? Tell me now before it's too late. I have the numbers on this paper!"

When no one else moved, his trick was unmasked. He had no numbers on the list, so to maintain his charade, he asked a *Wehrmacht* sergeant for the numbers of three prisoners who had done a poor job of working that day. Three prisoners were selected, and they were sent to the wall.

After the rest of the prisoners were dismissed for lunch, the eight men at the wall were told to turn around. Then they were handed a pickax and put through a two-hour regimen of exercises that required them to keep their arms outstretched holding the ax as they were ordered to squat, then to bend slowly left and right, repeating and repeating the process, all the while without any food. When their muscles tired, they were lashed on the face with whips. When they fell to the ground, they were kicked. When they passed out, they were revived with a bucket of water.

———————

What the photographs ultimately focused on was the Nazi concept of the *Untermensch,* a twisted, racist belief that the Jews (and many other peoples, including the Romany and Slavs) were inferior to the Nazi-termed Aryan race. Literally, *Untermensch* means "subhuman." And so Otto Kropf framed his photos in such a way as to highlight any imperfections in the prisoners. Israel Neumann was featured in eight of the photographs, three while standing at *Appell*. In the other five photos, Neumann and Abraham Feldberg struggled to carry a huge pot of soup to demonstrate the chore of *Essenholen*.

It was a perfect, self-fulfilling recipe for the Nazi belief in Jews as *Untermensch*: Take two short Jewish men, dress them as buffoons in oversize uniforms, give them an item that is too heavy to easily carry, and make them parade back and forth while a photographer snaps them in action.

Kropf, with the help of the Breendonk SS, manufactured exactly what the Nazis wanted to show.

Israel Neumann and Abraham Feldberg were chosen by the photographer Kropf to pose in a series of five pictures, struggling to carry a large pot of soup through the courtyard. (Top: Kropf photo 17) (Bottom: Kropf photo 20)

CAMP OF THE CREEPING DEATH

June 1941–June 1942

13

O PERATION SOLSTICE

A flyer distributed by members of the Independence Front warned German soldiers, "Hitler is your death."

A s the summer of 1941 began, life at Breendonk hit a new milestone.

On June 22, Germany expanded the war with its invasion of the Soviet Union. The governments of both countries had very different political beliefs and agendas, but they had maintained a nonaggression pact for almost two years. The Soviet Union had even supplied Germany with food and other resources, but now Hitler wanted more territory for his people, along with the natural resources that accompanied it, such as petroleum and iron ore.

This invasion meant a huge transformation at Breendonk. Until then, the number of prisoners at the camp fluctuated between 150 and 175 men. But on June 22, the SIPO-SD ordered the seizure of communists and communist sympathizers in an action called Operation Solstice; they were now considered political enemies of the Third Reich. Over 300 people—including 100 Soviet citizens living in Belgium—were arrested. More than half were sent to regular prisons, but 121 of them were taken to Breendonk.

Sixty of these prisoners, who were brought on the same truck, were conducted to the courtyard, where they stood at attention facing the wall for two hours. Then an SS officer confiscated their possessions and escorted them to an empty barrack, where they spent the night. They were awakened the next morning at four o'clock and returned to the courtyard for another two hours. Only then did the SS clerk register them, the barber shave their heads, and the tailor give them their uniforms. After that, they were sent to the work site.

Other, smaller, similar groups of prisoners were brought in during the weeks that followed, quickly doubling the camp's population.

On the morning of June 22, Adrien Henderickx was delivering underground anti-Nazi newspapers in a suburb of Brussels when he heard that Germany had attacked the Soviet Union and that the police were raiding the houses of suspected communists. He hurried home, where his neighbors warned him that the SIPO-SD had been searching for him. He quickly removed all the underground newspapers and pamphlets and destroyed a list of people who distributed them.

Shortly after, a policeman with a machine gun and agents from the SIPO-SD arrived and arrested him. When he tried to take some food from the kitchen to eat on his way to the police station, Henderickx was told that his interrogation would take no more than ten minutes. Instead, he was sent to Breendonk, where he was beaten, locked in a barrack with three dozen other new communist prisoners, and deprived of food for three days. This was just the beginning of his ordeal, which lasted some four years.

———

Pavel Koussonsky.

Russian by birth, sixty-one-year-old Pavel Koussonsky had been a general in the army of the White Russians, who were on the losing side of the Russian revolution in 1917. He left the country and eventually settled in Belgium. He, his family, and his friends believed that his arrest on June 22 had been a mistake, because he was not a communist at all. But the *Militärverwaltung* ordered the arrests of Russians as well as communists, without considering that there might be a difference between the two. His family attempted to secure his release by making a personal appeal to General von Falkenhausen, but they did not receive a timely response.

———

A Russian Jew, Isaac Lasareff was a doctor specializing in internal medicine. He had moved his family to Germany, but in 1933 they fled the anti-Semitism there and sought asylum in Belgium, where his immigrant status did not permit him to practice medicine. At sixty-four years of age, Lasareff was among the oldest prisoners taken to Breendonk that day.

Isaac Lasareff.

——————

René Blieck, a Brussels lawyer, had been under surveillance by the SIPO-SD since the end of 1940. Active in the initial stages of the Belgian resistance movement, he was a member of an underground communist organization called the Independence Front, which had been organized by a doctor, a journalist, and a Catholic priest. By the end of the war, the Front grew well beyond its political origins and became "a driving force in the battle" against the German occupation. Its members supplied false identity papers, planned and carried out sabotage, and helped many Belgians avoid compulsory labor deportations to Germany. They also printed and distributed 167 underground publications to keep the public informed about the occupier and to encourage resistance; most were just a page or two long and printed in small quantities. René Blieck was responsible for editing and circulating a few of these newspapers.

René Blieck.

At Breendonk, Blieck was assigned to be Jacques Ochs's workmate. By June 1941, Ochs had been removed from the blacksmith shop and had been given chores in the Room Service. He now cleaned the barracks and swept the courtyard, the hallways, and even the entrance tunnel that led to freedom. In addition, he tidied the rooms of the noncommissioned SS officers. Ochs and Blieck saw another side of prison life in the SS rooms: a bottle of cologne, books and newspapers to read, and even cigarette butts that they could hide in their socks to give to their friends.

Ochs was clearly impressed with Blieck, especially with his positive attitude, his intelligence, his excellent memory, and his love of poetry. Blieck, Ochs learned, had already published two volumes of his own poems. As they worked, Blieck would recite poetry that he had memorized. Ochs asked him to write down some of the poems so that he could learn them by heart as well.

One day, when the entire camp was being punished for a minor infraction, the memorized poetry came in handy. All the prisoners had been ordered to stand at attention in the courtyard for two straight hours. The only way Ochs could cope with this punishment was to distract himself in two ways. First, he counted to six hundred (which, he estimated, took ten minutes). Then he silently recited some of the poems that he had committed to memory from Blieck's transcriptions. By alternating the counting with the silent recitation, he made the two hours pass more quickly.

Ochs realized that Blieck had given him a gift: the power of poetry, even under the worst circumstances.

14

PRISONER
NUMBER 59

Hirsz and Eljasz Swirski, by Jacques Ochs.

The main tormentors at the camp during the first year—Prauss, Obler, and Lewin—seemed to prey on the weakest and most vulnerable inmates. On June 28, less than one week after Operation Solstice had swelled the ranks of Breendonk prisoners, they struck again; this time their target was Hirsz Swirski.

Eljasz Swirski, c. 1941.

Two Swirski brothers were imprisoned at Breendonk: twenty-one-year-old Eljasz and twenty-five-year-old Hirsz, both born in Poland. When Hirsz was arrested, Eljasz asked if he could accompany his brother to Breendonk in order to protect him. Hirsz was, according to Jacques Ochs, a "clumsy and simple-minded" young man. He had such a beautiful voice that he was called the *Sängerknabe,* or "choir boy." But *Zugführers* Obler and Lewin took a dislike to Hirsz and abused him.

He was not good at working or making his bed and was often deprived of breakfast and sometimes a whole day's food. In the end, he was beaten to death

Hirsz Swirski, c. 1933.

by *Zugführer* Lewin. Jacques Ochs retained the nightmarish memory of Swirski "lying on the pavement of the courtyard, eyes rolled back completely."

He was prisoner number 59.

Four days later, a new prisoner—Mozes Louft—arrived and was given Swirski's uniform to wear. He, too, would be number 59. The reuse of prisoner numbers and uniforms became a common practice at Breendonk; number 172 was reused at least six times.

Louft, a Jewish poultry seller in Antwerp, was arrested by the SIPO-SD because someone reported him for unspecified reasons. He had already spent three months in prison before his transfer to Breendonk.

Mozes Louft.

On July 4, two days after his arrival, *Oberarbeitsführer* Obler gave Louft a special job: he placed him on a boat that resembled a small barge and told him to cut the tall grass that had grown up along the edges of the moat. The boat was often used by outside workers to ferry cement and gravel across the moat to the fort.

Then something happened.

Louft may not have been able to control the boat, or the breeze or a current may have pushed it too far away from the fort. Some suggested that Louft's wife, Rajzla Bicher, had come to watch him, as many loved ones did, from the other side of the moat, outside the camp perimeter.

Some said that he raised his hand to wave to her.

What occurred next, though, was not in doubt: A *Wehrmacht* soldier named Benninger took aim and shot Louft twice. Jacques Ochs, who was in one of the barrack rooms at the time, heard the sound and looked out the window. Not long after, he saw some men carrying a bloody body through the courtyard.

The prisoners who had been working outside told everyone that Louft had done nothing wrong. They knew the simple truth: he had been murdered.

––––––––

July 4 was also Frans Fischer's first day as a prisoner at the camp. Forty-eight-year-old Fischer, a former member of the Belgian parliament, had been arrested on June 22 for expressing anti-Nazi political opinions.

That night, he and other prisoners were suddenly awakened, then told to get dressed and line up outside. When they were in position in the courtyard, SS-Lieutenant Prauss addressed the men, "A villain tried to escape. Justice has been done, and I commend the brave *Wehrmacht* soldier who has done his duty."

He added, "If any among you is considering an escape attempt, you are going to see what awaits you."

What awaited them was Louft's fate.

They were told to form a single line and head to the right, where they had to file past Louft's body. It was "completely naked, thrown on the ground—legs curled up, hands outstretched to the sky, eyes wide open, lying in a large pool of blood. On each side of the victim, the major and the lieutenant [stood] in the affected pose of the triumphant gladiator."

One prisoner, a Brussels barber, looked away when he

Prisoners filing past the body of Mozes Louft, by Jacques Ochs.

passed the body. An SS corporal stopped him and thrust the man's head within inches of Louft's face. "Look . . . with your eyes wide open."

After the men were sent back to bed, Fischer was selected for a special duty. As a new prisoner, he was given cleaning equipment and ordered to mop up the blood from the courtyard.

———

In the days that followed, Benninger, the soldier who had shot Louft, boasted to the prisoners about his accomplishment. He showed them his ammunition belt, which had held twelve cartridges; two were missing.

"You see . . . I still have another ten. Whose turn is it now?"

Some came to believe that Louft had been murdered to serve as a warning to obey the rules, especially since so many new prisoners had recently arrived.

Hermann Kahn.

Whatever the reason, the rumor soon spread that Benninger had received a special leave for killing Louft.

———

Six days later, Hermann Kahn arrived at Breendonk. He, too, was given prisoner number 59. He survived a year and a half at Breendonk before he was sent elsewhere.

15

A SUBSTITUTION

The SS took over an apartment building on Avenue Louise in Brussels and turned it into the headquarters of the SIPO-SD.

Not long after Isaac Lasareff was arrested during Operation Solstice, his wife sent their son, Vladimir, a postcard informing him that his father had fallen gravely ill and had been sent to a clinic. She did not dare write the truth because she knew that agents from the SIPO-SD might read her mail. Vladimir, however, realized right away that the coded message meant his father had been imprisoned.

A physicist at the University of Liège, he hurried to his parents' home in Brussels to find out more information, but his mother had no idea where Isaac had been taken. So Vladimir, perhaps without considering the consequences, decided to go directly to the Brussels headquarters of the SIPO-SD.

Vladimir Lasareff.

He spoke first to a civilian worker, who asked, "Your father, is he Jewish?"

"Yes."

"And your mother?"

"Also."

"Then how dare you, a one hundred per-cent Jew, expect to get any information from the secret police?"

The man slammed the door in Lasareff's face, but the physicist persisted. He was finally admitted to the office of an SS lieutenant, who revealed that his father had been taken to a camp.

"Where is the camp?"

"Somewhere," the officer replied vaguely.

"Why was my father arrested?"

"That's our business."

"Can I go see him?"

"Yes. . . . Be at your mother's house tomorrow morning. . . . I will come looking for you."

The next day, Lasareff waited, but the SS lieutenant never arrived. Frustrated, he returned to the SIPO-SD headquarters the following day and again spoke to the officer, who explained that he had had to postpone his trip. He promised to pick him up the next day. Once more, the officer did not materialize, so Lasareff returned to the headquarters.

The officer was not pleased to see Lasareff.

"Have you gone crazy, you damned Jewish scum? How dare you disturb us in such a shameless way. Do you really want to see your father? . . . Well . . . you will see him soon. And since it irritates me greatly . . . to release your father, . . . you will take his place."

With that, Lasareff's wish was granted, but at great cost to him. The officer arranged for a driver and three guards to escort him to the camp. They drove halfway toward Antwerp before the driver exited the asphalt highway and headed down a brick-colored dirt road surrounded by barren hills. It was only then that the three guards voiced the destination: "Breendonk."

Lasareff had never heard the word before.

"I knew nothing of the camp, except that my father was imprisoned there," he wrote after the war. "I knew nothing of what happened there. But a moment later, I knew. . . . Because I saw on the hills . . . groups of men, shirtless, wielding . . . large shovels. Others pushed . . . wheelbarrows full of earth. In many places German sentries were posted."

The car passed under the barricade and parked in the square in front of the fort. SS-Lieutenant Prauss approached the car and accompanied Lasareff inside the fort to the courtyard. There, he saw an old man dressed in a Belgian army uniform, his head shaved, his body shrunken, his face full of deep wrinkles, his hands with open wounds, his cheeks covered in tears.

"It was my father," Lasareff realized finally, "unrecognizable after eighteen days' imprisonment."

As he reached for his father's hands, Vladimir's face was slammed against the stucco wall. When he tried to turn his head to look at his father, he was struck on the back. Then his father was led away to freedom, replaced by his son. Vladimir was given the same uniform, the same bed in the same barrack, and the same number: 141.

———————

The next day, he was assigned to push a wheelbarrow. After ten trips, he was exhausted, but he could tell from the position of the sun that it was still early morning. He continued to work but his body rebelled: his muscles burned and his eyes ached from the sun's glare. Worst of all, his feet were on fire. The old military boots that he had been given did not fit well. With every step, his skin rubbed against the hard leather. No matter how he tried to walk, he could not avoid the pain.

Finally, when he couldn't walk any more, another prisoner advised him to fall down next to his wheelbarrow and pretend to be unconscious. Although the guards would beat him, they would leave him alone afterward until it was time for the *Appell* before lunch.

He chose a place to fall and collapsed onto the ground. Only then did he realize that he was so tired and in such pain that if the guards beat him, he would not have the strength to protect himself. Other prisoners crowded around him, and when the guards approached screaming, the prisoners told them that he had sunstroke. Instead of beating him, the guards ordered some men to drag him to a nearby pile of stones, where he was able to rest until lunch.

———————

Vladimir Lasareff would have been standing on one of the sandy hills in the background when SS-Lieutenant Arthur Prauss decided to reprimand him. (Kropf photo 25)

Like many of the prisoners at Breendonk, Lasareff harbored the idea that he would be freed from the camp in a few days. Around the same time each day, Prauss or another officer would call the numbers of the prisoners who were going to be released.

One day, as he was shoveling one of the sand hills that covered the roof of the fort, Lasareff heard Prauss call his number. Certain that he would be let go, he stumbled painfully down the hill toward Prauss. By now, the heels of his feet were infected and inflamed with pus-filled sores.

"One forty-one, why aren't you working?" Prauss asked him.

"But I am working, Herr Lieutenant."

"I'm telling you that you are not working."

"I am working according to my ability," Lasareff explained.

"Here, you don't work according to your ability, but according to my wishes."

With that, Prauss slapped Lasareff's cheek with his gloved hand, daring him to fight back. Instead, Lasareff turned and began to climb the hill again. As he reached the top, Prauss called to him again, forcing Lasareff to make his way back down the hill.

"How dare you waste time by returning to work so slowly," Prauss complained.

"I can't walk . . . any faster. . . . My leg is very sore."

Prauss was livid and ready to pounce, but Lasareff's unnamed *Zugführer,* who had been listening nearby, tackled him first. He threw him on the ground and pretended to beat him. At the same time, he whispered in his ear, "If you want to live, you'd better make sure you climb that hill running."

Lasareff realized that the advice might save his life and help him see his family again. He climbed the hill as fast as he could, fast enough to prevent Prauss from complaining more. But the sores on his feet continued to fester.

16

THE RIVALS

Léon Degrelle with his family.

On July 21, Belgians normally celebrated National Day, the date that their first king took his oath after Belgium won its independence from the Netherlands in 1831. But in 1941, the *Militärverwaltung* prohibited all patriotic activities that day, with one exception.

Members of Rex, a Fascist political party whose leaders had chosen to collaborate with the military administration, had been given permission to celebrate the holiday publicly in Brussels. Led by Léon Degrelle, who hoped to be selected by the Germans as the new Belgium *Führer* under Nazi rule, Rex had an estimated 20,000 members in 1940, primarily in the French-speaking part of Belgium. Although Degrelle would do almost anything to curry favor with the Germans, he did not seem to realize that as Rex became more aligned with Nazi ideology, most Belgians considered its members to be traitors to their country.

The police realized that a Rexist celebration on National Day would not be well received by the Belgian public, but they were ready with a trap for any protesters. As Rexists paraded that day, someone in the crowd shouted "Long Live Belgium," spurring a counterdemonstration. The police attacked; many men were arrested and sent to Breendonk.

As the large group arrived, they were forced to run down the tunnel to the courtyard between a gauntlet of *Wehrmacht* soldiers, who kicked and hit them with their fists and rifle butts. They stood at the wall for hours, where many were beaten again.

From July 21 to 23, about seventy new prisoners arrived. Most had been involved in protests, but at least ten of them fit a new subcategory of prisoner: they were *hostages,* well-known men who had not committed a crime. Among them were political leaders, prosecutors, a policeman, and one bar owner named Louis Bamps. Like the others, Bamps was unsure why he had been arrested. He wondered if it was because he had staged his own protest on National Day by wearing the colors of the Belgian flag. But he and the other nine soon learned that they were being held as a result of recent bombings that had taken place against the Germans. The SIPO-SD threatened to begin executing hostages in the hope that such a reprisal would prevent further violence by resistance groups.

———————

As a result of the various crackdowns from June through mid-September, at least 337 new prisoners were sent to Breendonk, bringing the total population to 450. Because the barracks would be insufficient if more prisoners arrived, a new wing of four temporary barracks, built of wood on the side of the west courtyard, was begun. Termed the Jewish barracks, they would house both Jews and non-Jews in separate rooms. Room 1, which had been reserved for Jews until then, would eventually be used for other purposes.

Another problem related to the huge increase in prisoners was the inadequate facilities for personal hygiene, already a difficult issue at Breendonk. There were still only eight toilets, but they were now used by 450 prisoners. To improve the situation, an open barrel with an eight-foot diameter had been installed in each courtyard so that twelve men at one time could squat over each one, their rears practically touching, and relieve themselves. In a span of just a minute or two, each prisoner had to undress, take care of his personal needs, and readjust his clothing—all the time while prisoners lined up waiting their turn and guards watched their every move. Only in October 1943 was a large room with more than fifty toilets finally constructed.

Many prisoners could not function under these conditions. Since they were only taken to the toilet twice a day, some preferred to wait until they were at work to ask for permission

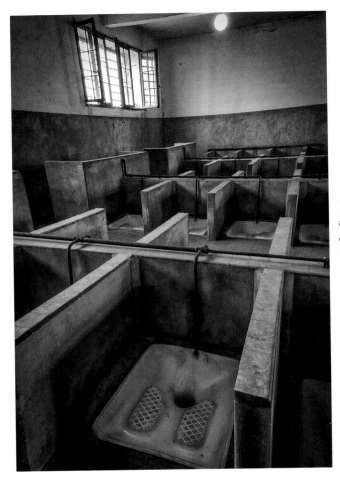

The toilet room was completed in October 1943.

to use the toilet. Even then, they had to follow a special procedure. Holding his cap in his right hand, a prisoner had to stand
at attention, about ten feet from the guard, and ask, "Sir sentry,
I ask you most respectfully to be allowed to leave for a while."
Some preferred this, though, since there could be more pri-
vacy and less pressure.

Showering was also traumatic. Even though a large room
with sixty-four showers had been added to the northeast
corner of the fort that summer, the camp administration insisted
that all Breendonk prisoners had to have their one weekly
shower within one particular hour every Saturday. This meant

that thirty-two prisoners at a time were herded into a twenty-foot-square changing room and given only a few minutes to shower, all the while being told by the guards to hurry.

Even if prisoners could tune out the incessant commands, they could not stop the guards from amusing themselves by turning the water temperature from hot to cold whenever it pleased them.

————

Overcrowding also led to more overt friction between prisoners, especially in the barracks. As Paul Lévy described it, the guards would tell Jewish prisoners, "You are only Jews. . . . For this you suffer. But you are guilty of nothing else. So show the Aryans that you are able to have cleaner barracks and better-made beds." On the other hand, the same guards would tell non-Jewish prisoners, "You, the pure ones, you fought stupidly against us. Look at those dirty Jews, those vile beings have succeeded in teaching you a lesson. Your 'Bettenbau'—your bed making—is worth nothing in comparison to them!" Lévy summarized the guards' attempts to stir trouble in four words: "Divide. Prevail. Compare. Harass."

Tension also existed because the Jewish and non-Jewish prisoners were prejudiced against each other. Frans Fischer displayed his own contempt one day on the work site. As a single file of prisoners carried heavy loads of rubble to the top of a hill one day, Fischer was unhappy with the slow Jewish man in front of him "who, dragging his leg, delayed the progress of the column."

The *Zugführer* behind Fischer was annoyed as well, and began to hit Fischer with his truncheon. Fischer did not want to be beaten, but he especially did not want to be beaten by a man who "wore the distinctive yellow band of the Israelite people on his jacket."

When an SS officer walked by moments later, Fischer

The SS at Breendonk wagered on the teams of prisoners who pushed carts. (Left: Kropf photo 34) (Right: Kropf photo 35)

asked him, "Can a Jewish *Zugführer* hit an Aryan prisoner?"

The question surprised the officer. After a moment, he replied, "Of course not. Is this the one who hit you?"

Fischer nodded.

The officer then grabbed a truncheon from a nearby guard and handed it to Fischer.

"Hit him as many times as he hit you!" the officer said.

Fischer thought better about his impulsive behavior and declined the offer. But his apparent anti-Semitism was not unique among the non-Jewish prisoners.

Similarly, Paul Lévy, a practicing Catholic who was assigned to the predominantly Jewish Room 1, felt uncomfortable when he made the sign of the cross before and after meals or before getting up and going to bed. He wanted to practice his

religion "without thirty-one pairs of eyes watching [him as if he were] a strange and hostile beast." He felt like an intruder who was called a Jew by the Nazis but refused to be one.

One of his friends from Room 1, Ben Galanter, explained that his Jewish roommates did not understand the sign of the cross under their present circumstances. He told Lévy, "For them, that which is not Jewish is Christian and everyone else— even the SS—are Christians in their eyes. These are 'Christians' who ostracized them from society. . . . When you make the sign, for them, it's the sign of their torturers, even if you know that these SS are the most anti-Christian of the anti-Christians!"

Lévy decided that because he was a Christian, he could not cause such anguish. He stopped making the sign of the cross for the rest of his time at Breendonk.

17

THE PLANT EATERS

The food ration at the camp became even more severe during
the summer of 1941.

The prisoners of the overcrowded camp faced another problem that summer when food packages from relatives were suddenly prohibited. SS-Lieutenant Prauss listed the reasons for the ban: letters, money, tobacco, and even communist propaganda had supposedly been found in some packages, hidden inside loaves of bread or jars of jam. Most prisoners thought this was just an excuse to deprive them further.

Family members often came to the camp with a food package for their loved one. They would go to the main entrance and leave the package with the sentry, although it was rarely delivered, even when no ban was in effect. After handing over the package, family members would linger beyond the camp perimeter, watching, waiting, hoping to see their relative. One father was even said to bring binoculars so that he might spy his son more clearly.

But it would be trouble for a prisoner if he acknowledged his relative and was noticed by a guard. He might be beaten or placed in a solitary-confinement cell and even locked in leg irons as a punishment. Beyond that, as one prisoner noted, when a prisoner caught a glimpse of a loved one, rather than feeling better, he often became terribly depressed.

With the reduction in rations and the ban on food packages, prisoners found themselves "hungry from every pore." Breendonk became a camp of starvation, or as some prisoners came to call it, a camp of the creeping death.

The one slice of bread that was breakfast and dinner was a special type of indestructible bread meant for soldiers in the field, concocted so that it would not go bad very quickly. The soup at lunch was still thin and insubstantial.

When Louis Bamps entered the tailor workshop on July 23 to receive his uniform, the portly man was told by the

At least one solitary-confinement cell had permanent leg irons.

Frydmans that they did not have pants large enough to fit him properly. The pair they gave him were too snug. "It will fit in about a week," he was assured, indicating that the strict diet of the camp would cause him to lose weight rapidly. When he received his first Breendonk dinner that night—a ladle of brown water that masqueraded as coffee and a slice of soldier's bread—he understood what they meant.

As the summer of famine continued, prisoners would sit around in their free time during the evening and talk about what they would eat when they gained their release: Belgian fries, omelets, steaks, and more. As they imagined the elaborate menu of their fantasy feasts, their "hollow cheeks . . . grew purple with a feverish flush, their voices began to tremble, their eyes filled with tears." But such dreams were really tortured nightmares, for they did not know when they might be liberated.

The suffering of three prisoners, by Jacques Ochs.

So they began to improvise. Prisoners on kitchen duty who had to peel potatoes tried to stuff a few in their uniform pockets. Others would wander by the pigsty or the rabbit hutch looking for scraps of food meant for the animals. On the work site, they would scavenge for anything to eat, such as an edible root or herb. Even a dandelion became a valued ingredient that could be stirred into a bowl of lunchtime soup. At least once, hatchlings in a bird's nest were gobbled up whole when they were discovered. Prisoners were also on the lookout for frogs and mice, which they would also eat on the spot.

Adrien Henderickx, arrested during Operation Solstice, noticed that the camp cook carried buckets of food scraps to the pigsty around the same time each day. Since this occurred while he was working, Henderickx made a point to ask the guard if he could use the toilet during that time. If permission was given, he would wander by the pigsty on his way. One day he pocketed potato peels, some greens, and a large bone from the floor of the pigsty. He shared the bone with three friends; each one could gnaw on the bone for a day before passing it to the next person. In that way, the bone lasted five days.

Another day, however, some prisoners spied Henderickx scavenging for scraps. Also anxious for food, they descended on the pigsty in such a frenzy that the pigs escaped and ran squealing through the courtyards. The men quickly dispersed, but SS-Major Schmitt and SS-Lieutenant Prauss soon learned of the problem and ordered an *Appell*. With Lump at his side, sniffing for remnants of the pigs' food, Schmitt inspected each man's hands for evidence that he had participated in the theft. Seven men, including Henderickx, were implicated; the rest were sent to their barracks.

Then Schmitt asked the seven men in an unusually quiet voice, "Why did you do that? You know that it was the food . . . for our pigs."

Although the men did not want to reply, they knew that the guards were ready to beat them. So they told Schmitt the truth: they stole the food because they were hungry.

In a voice seemingly filled with pity, Schmitt replied, "We Germans . . . understand very well that you must be hungry, so I'm going to give you some extra food now."

The men were rightly suspicious of his intentions when he took them to the kitchen, where the lunchtime soup was still being prepared. Schmitt told the cook to ladle two bowls of the boiling soup for each man.

"If you're really hungry," he told them, "I need you to prove it to me by drinking immediately and without stopping the broth that I have offered you out of the goodness of my heart." Guards stationed behind them were instructed to whip them if they paused before each bowl was emptied.

The men had no choice but to comply. The hot soup

scalded their mouths and throats and stomachs. Afterward, Schmitt told the men that he wanted them to be able to better digest their extra meal, so they were escorted to the courtyard for two hours of grueling exercise.

———

Other desperate, starving prisoners would lie on the ground at the work site and become *Grünfresser,* or plant eaters. The work site was hilly, and the guards could not always see every prisoner at one time. If a prisoner was caught eating grass, he was punished. One prisoner, Hector Urbain, reportedly died from eating grass that summer; his death certificate read "inflammation of the stomach and intestine from eating grass."

However, Adrien Henderickx was with him that day. They were digging with their shovels when they came across some earthworms. "Blinded by hunger," Henderickx later wrote, "I put some in my pocket to mix into my soup . . . at lunch." Urbain, however, immediately ate the worms raw, and died a short time later. Henderickx believed that the worms killed him.

———

Some days, in another ongoing act of cruelty, the guards lined the prisoners up in the courtyard before lunch and made them empty their pockets. Anyone who had collected even one blade of grass, let alone a dandelion or a daisy or a clump of clover, to add to his soup was forced to stand at the wall for an hour, delaying his lunch. One day, a prisoner succeeded in catching a small fish about the size of a sardine in the moat. He had tucked it safely into his pocket, but during the surprise inspection, Prauss discovered it and angrily threw the fish onto the ground and crushed it with his boot. The man faced the wall for an hour.

One night, the prisoners in Room 1 were taken outside after dinner and given the chore of peeling potatoes as an act of cruel temptation. Three large bags of potatoes were emptied onto the cobblestones of the courtyard. As the prisoners worked, they were carefully guarded by the *Wehrmacht* soldiers. Then, when they had finished, the soldiers took the potatoes and the peelings and weighed them. Next, they announced that more than sixty pounds of potatoes were missing.

A prisoner beaten by a Wehrmacht soldier, by Jacques Ochs.

As a result, the prisoners were made to run across the courtyard, lie down, and stand up and run again, then crawl across the courtyard, their heads down, their feet stretched out, using only their elbows to move. Prisoners in their barracks watched through their windows as the men were repeatedly struck with roof tiles and rifle butts and kicked in the head and body. The abuse lasted an hour.

Sometimes a prisoner was so consumed by hunger that he would lose all scruples and attempt to steal food from another inmate. Paul Lévy knew that the man in the bunk next to him—Lévy referred to him as "J," but it was most likely Jürgen Jacobsohn—had stolen some potatoes as he helped unload a truck of foodstuffs one day. Those potatoes were hidden under Jacobsohn's pillow; every night, Lévy saw him count and recount his precious hoard.

One day, when Jacobsohn was not present, Lévy placed his hand under the pillow to see if the potatoes were still

Jürgen Jacobsohn, by Jacques Ochs.

there. He realized that this was a dangerous temptation, for once he felt the rough and dusty skin between his fingers he knew he would have to take one and eat it. He couldn't stop himself from stealing a potato; it tasted delicious.

That night, Jacobsohn found that his potato hoard had been raided.

"Which one of you is the pig . . . who steals from his friends? Which one is the pig who dares to lay his hands on the property of a poor unfortunate man?" Jacobsohn asked the other prisoners in Room 1.

Lévy felt so guilty that he imagined all the other prisoners' eyes were watching him. As a devout Catholic, he decided to confess to the crime, but he wasn't sure whom he should tell. Finally, he chose *Zugführer* Obler.

"Obler, Mr. Obler," he began sheepishly, " . . . the potato
. . . ? Well, it's me."

Obler's reaction to the confession surprised Lévy.

He looked at Lévy and said, "You did it, too?"

They both had stolen a potato from Jacobsohn.

The realization that he was no better than Obler motivated Lévy to avoid giving in to such temptation at Breendonk
again.

18

JULY 24, 1941

A prisoner with wheelbarrow, by Jacques Ochs.

J uly 24 was the first time that two prisoners were murdered on the same day.

It was also Louis Bamps's first day of work outdoors, where he had been assigned to push a wheelbarrow. As he waited for another prisoner to fill it with sand, he observed the man struggling to lift his shovel. He was in obvious pain; his head had been bandaged from repeated beatings. But the agony caused by each movement, no matter how small, was too much, and the man collapsed.

Schyja Dolinger.

The episode was seared into Bamps's memory, and he wrote about it after the war.

One of the *Arbeitsführers* seemed to have been waiting for the man to falter and ran over "ranting and raving. . . . His truncheon whizzed through the air and came down violently on the head of the unfortunate man. I saw how the blood trickled from his ear, a skull fracture." Then an unnamed *Zugführer* walked over and poured a bucket of cold water on the unconscious man, who then took a breath and shivered. Next, some prisoners were ordered to carry the man to the *Revier,* where he died, according to Dr. Köchling's report, of intestinal paralysis at four p.m.

Although Bamps did not know the name of the man beaten to death on the work site that day, camp records indicated that it was Schyja Dolinger, a Jew who had escaped from Nazi Germany a few months after *Kristallnacht.*

Israel Neumann, 1930.

———

The second man to die that day was Israel Neumann.

Like Hirsz Swirski, who had been murdered less than a month earlier, Neumann could not make his bed according to the strict *Bettenbau* standards because he was clumsy. As a result, he often went without breakfast. When assigned to *Essenholen* duty, he sometimes spilled the soup on the way back to the room. With his short legs, he was unable to march in long steps to keep up with the rest of the prisoners when they did their military drills for Prauss. According to Paul Lévy, he did not know the difference between left and right.

The SS made him the laughingstock of the camp. When visitors came to tour Breendonk at the invitation of the SS or the SIPO-SD, Neumann "was used as a

Israel Neumann was singled out by SS-photographer Otto Kropf in this propaganda photo taken in June 1941. (Kropf photo 12)

puppet by the staff who had him dancing . . . or singing." To the *Zugführer* Walter Obler, though, he was anything but amusing. Neumann stood in the way of Obler attaining a perfect barrack.

So Obler punished him.

He deprived him of food.

He slapped and kicked and beat him.

———

All the while, Jacques Ochs drew his portrait.

Some of the portraits were serious; others were caricatures that exaggerated his physical features. A number of the caricatures seemed to perpetuate the Nazi stereotype of the *Untermensch*. Some historians have wondered if this

Israel Neumann and Ludwig Juliusberger, by Jacques Ochs.

reflected Ochs's own possible anti-Semitism, or if it was his attempt to give Commandant Schmitt exactly what he wanted. After all, Ochs was trying to save his own life. Whatever his motive, his serious drawings of Neumann captured the overwhelming isolation that the man must have felt at the camp.

———

After the war, Ochs wrote a brief account of Neumann's death. Obler, a giant of a man next to Neumann, reportedly picked him up much like a doll, lifted him horizontally over his head, and threw him to the ground one day. According to Ochs, this caused his death.

Vladimir Lasareff provided a more detailed account of Neumann's death. In the days before July 24, Lasareff needed medical attention for the terrible sores on his feet and went to see the doctor outside the *Revier*. That is when he encountered a man whom he called "little Isaac"—in fact, the man was Israel Neumann. Perhaps Neumann had already been thrown to the ground by Obler, for Lasareff saw him slumped down in the hallway, unable to stand upright.

Suddenly, SS-Major Schmitt and his dog, Lump, approached. Everyone jumped to attention, except Neumann.

"Will you stand up immediately?" Schmitt yelled at him.

Neumann said nothing and simply looked up at the officer. Schmitt took his whip and thrashed it repeatedly against Neumann's shoulders. Neumann tried to stand up but was knocked back to the floor. Schmitt continued to beat his hands, his ears, his face. All the while, Lump tore at him, ripping his clothes.

As he witnessed this scene, Lasareff remembered wishing that Neumann would be lucky enough to die from the beating. No prisoner in the hallway that day could help him, or he would have been beaten too. Attracted by Lump's barking, SS-Lieutenant Prauss and *Zugführer* Lewin soon came to watch the spectacle. Lewin began kicking Neumann's sprawled body, an action that might reward him with an extra piece of bread at dinner. Eventually, the beating stopped and the tormentors moved on. Neumann, still alive, was admitted to the *Revier.*

The next time he saw Neumann, a few days later, Lasareff was in the *Revier* himself, placed in a bed adjacent to him. Neumann never opened his eyes; his only movement was his breathing.

On July 24, though, he cried out hoarsely, "Herr Lieutenant, let me write to my wife!"

These were the only spoken words of Neumann that were ever recorded at Breendonk. No one except Lasareff heard the plea, but he knew that Prauss would have denied the request.

———

Israel Neumann died at about six o'clock on the evening of July 24.

As his emaciated body lay in the *Revier,* Prauss entered and grinned at the sight of the corpse.

Then he said, *Er sieht aus wie ein Affe.* "He looks like a monkey."

That momentary encounter, according to Jacques Ochs, was the only funeral Neumann received, and the sentence uttered by Prauss his only eulogy. He was pronounced dead by Dr. Singer that day; Dr. Köchling examined the body the next morning at 10:45 and noted the cause of death. Israel Neumann had died of a heart attack.

Shortly before Neumann's death, Jacques Ochs sketched a more serious and reflective drawing of him.

THE HELL
OF BREENDONK

A beating, by Jacques Ochs.

Almost every day that summer, new victims were selected for abuse.

On August 20, some prisoners witnessed a terrible beating after dinner when a man was chased through the courtyard by a group of soldiers. They slammed him to the ground, then hit him. Over the course of an hour, they repeated the process: chasing him, flattening him, and beating him. The prisoners could only watch in helpless horror. Finally, the soldiers made him stand against the wall, where the beating continued. A short time later, when he backed away from the wall moaning and staggering, a soldier was ready with a bucket of liquid manure and dumped it on his head.

All the while, the soldiers laughed.

The camp logbook indicated that Eugène Jacob was taken to the military hospital in Antwerp around that date; he died there on August 22. The fifty-six-year-old man, a Jewish shopkeeper from Arlon who was arrested around the same time as Abraham Feldberg, was most likely the prisoner beaten that night. Both Jacques Ochs and Abraham Feldberg mentioned after the war that Jacob was suffering from starvation and beatings at the time of his death.

Eugène Jacob, by Jacques Ochs.

Many inmates would do anything possible to avoid such treatment, but punishments were often arbitrary and unpredictable. The former general Pavel Koussonsky, one of the Operation Solstice prisoners, was too proud *not* to be beaten.

As an older man, Koussonsky struggled at the work site, but he stubbornly refused to ask for lesser chores. Instead of breaking rocks, which was considered the easiest outdoor job, he persisted in pushing the wheelbarrow. When he couldn't keep up the rapid pace, he was beaten by SS-Lieutenant Prauss or *Oberarbeitsführer* Obler. By the end of August, the beatings had taken their toll.

Boris Solonevitch, another Russian prisoner, who arrived on the same day as Koussonsky, watched the old general being repeatedly hit about the face. Koussonsky stoically stood his ground and "fixed his eyes straight ahead, beyond his tormentors, as if they were only empty space." Only his quivering lips and bright red face betrayed the anger and humiliation that he felt.

Worried about the former general, Solonevitch made a secret visit to the *Revier* to speak to Dr. Singer. Solonevitch asked him to save Koussonsky, but Singer replied that the general's only hope of being admitted to the hospital was to collapse on the work site. "[If] he continues to work," the doctor warned, "I can do nothing for him."

Solonevitch told the general about the conversation and pleaded with him to follow the doctor's advice. Koussonsky declined, saying, "I cannot accept that a lieutenant general of the Russian Imperial Army is defeated, not because he lacks the strength, but because he feigned . . . a disease! . . . I have never feigned an illness or resorted to such tricks in my life, and I never will . . . even to the point of death. As long as I can stand up, I am staying with the others."

Prisoners at Breendonk sorting and breaking rocks.
(Kropf photo 29)

On the day before he died, Koussonsky could barely breathe, his face was flushed, his arms and legs were swollen, and a large bruised area on his face—the result of a beating with a truncheon—oozed pus. Even then, the suffering Koussonsky tried to put his heart into the meaningless labor. The next morning, when he could not move, he was taken to the *Revier*, where he died at 12:15 p.m. on August 26.

Koussonsky's death, however, created a problem for the *Militärverwaltung*. During July and August, twelve men, including the general, had died at Breendonk. Because of this high number and because Koussonsky had some influential friends, the military administration suddenly became interested in inspecting the camp. A cursory earlier examination, performed on July 25, had concluded that reports about the suffering of the prisoners were exaggerated. The recent deaths, however, seemed to show otherwise.

Josef Rormann.

A more thorough inspection was done September 9. During this visit, the inspectors stopped at the *Revier,* where some prisoners had been admitted for starvation edema. Their report determined that "an extended stay [at Breendonk] will in all probability lead to death." The inspection also uncovered another complaint—the supervision and abuse of non-Jewish prisoners by the Jewish *Arbeitsführers* Obler and Lewin.

The same day as the inspection, SS-Lieutenant Prauss and *Zugführer* Obler were out for blood. They found forty-six-year-old prisoner Josef Rormann, who was barely alive. Rormann, whose skeletal frame was swimming in his old uniform and whose "sunken eyes glowed with fever," was on his way to the *Revier.*

"Suddenly, in front of him appeared the lieutenant," Jacques Ochs recalled, "accompanied by the monster Obler. . . . The two brutes beat him with all their might." Later that afternoon, at the five p.m. *Appell,* Rormann was barely able to stand up. As Prauss instructed the prisoners to remove their hats, he noticed that Rormann could not comply. Sixteen times Rormann failed to remove his hat, until Prauss pulled

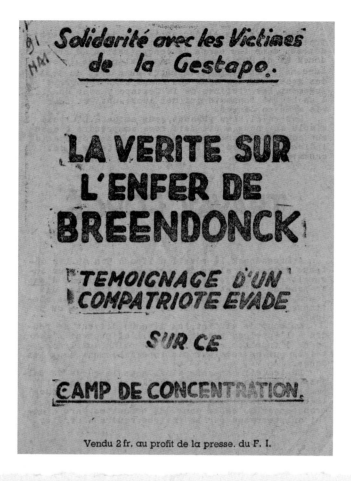

A flyer by the Independence Front provided information about the "Hell of Breendonk" by an escaped prisoner.

him out of line and ordered a seventeen-year-old *Zugführer* named Otto John to beat the man with a truncheon. He also set Lump on Rormann, and the dog tore into his calf.

When Prauss was satisfied with the punishment, Rormann was carried to the *Revier,* but by eight o'clock that night he was returned to his barrack. The next morning, he was dead.

The *Militärverwaltung* never knew of this episode.

———

After this inspection, senior officers of the *Militärverwaltung* decided to clean up Breendonk. Despite their signed pledges not to do so, prisoners released from the camp had reported their experiences, and the camp had become known as "the Hell of Breendonk." The military administration feared that such a reputation might make Belgians reluctant to collaborate, which in turn would affect productivity and the Germans' ability to exploit the country economically. To prevent this, they wanted to increase rations and prevent any Jewish prisoners from supervising and abusing non-Jews.

For its part, the SIPO-SD also wanted its own changes at Breendonk, primarily to replace the *Wehrmacht* soldiers with SS guards to strengthen the discipline at the overpopulated camp. By mid-September, therefore, members of the Flemish SS were brought to Breendonk to guard prisoners and perform some administrative duties.

But there were even more changes in store.

20

THE FIRST
TRANSPORT

Willebroek Rail Station.

On September 17, a decision was made to reduce the population of the camp. Prisoners realized that something unusual was happening when 105 of the weakest were suddenly confined to their barracks and not permitted to work. Their soup became a little thicker, and their bread ration was supplemented by about two additional ounces.

On September 21, Schmitt and Prauss toured the barracks with a group of high-ranking SS officers, who announced that the recuperating prisoners were going to be released. Among those on the list were the poet René Blieck and Adrien Henderickx.

Most had arrived at the camp between Operation Solstice and National Day. But one prisoner had been at the camp from the first day: René Dillen. The secretary of the Young Flemish Communist organization, he was unrecognizable to some of his friends who arrived at the camp that summer. "The man could barely move, was tremendously weakened and was completely gray" at twenty-eight years of age. Although everyone was starving at Breendonk, Dillen's condition seemed so much worse that a few of his friends set aside some of their food to give to him, in the hope of saving him.

The chosen men were ecstatic. They were called to the office to retrieve their belongings and their civilian clothes. They didn't care that their clothes had become moldy; they were happy to change out of their Breendonk uniforms. To gain their release, all they had to do was sign the standard pledge not to discuss their imprisonment at the camp. This, for freedom, they did willingly.

Then they were permitted to mingle in the courtyard with the *Wehrmacht* soldiers. It was a surreal scene, almost as if nothing terrible had ever happened. Of course, the other prisoners who had not been chosen for release were still on the work site and still being beaten. Their cries could be heard from time to time.

Next, the prisoners to be freed were each given a little more than half a pound of bread and a quarter pound of sausage and told to eat it sparingly, for it was all the food that they would have until they arrived home. Perhaps that should have been a sign that something was not right, but if this worried anyone, no record of their concerns was made. Finally, they were told that they were not going to be released that day, so they were housed in empty barrack rooms overnight, away from the other prisoners.

———

The next morning, they were ordered to line up in columns of five across. Flanked by *Wehrmacht* soldiers, some carrying rifles with fixed bayonets and others reining in guard dogs, they were marched a few kilometers down the road to the train station in Willebroek. No residents dared to peer out their windows at the unusual and unexpected sight.

At the station, the men were placed in train cars, some even in first-class compartments, and sent on their way. The shades in all the cars were drawn, so that the prisoners could not see where they were going. According to one account, the train went six miles east to Mechelen, then fifteen miles north to Antwerp, then back to Mechelen. At that point, the men would not have known what was happening.

Next, the train headed east . . . toward Germany. At the border, the train stopped and another train—this one with cattle cars containing four hundred other prisoners from a Belgian prison named Huy—was attached. Then the train moved slowly into Germany, stopping, sometimes waiting hours on isolated sidings, before resuming its journey.

In Adrien Henderickx's car, the ten Jews placed on the transport were tormented by the guards. Lined up in the aisle,

An unknown person took this forbidden photograph of a Breendonk transport before it departed from the Willebroek train station.

they were forced to exercise by standing on their tiptoes, with their arms outstretched, then squatting, jumping forward, again and again, "like toads." Anyone whose leg muscles gave out and stopped jumping was beaten about the head with a whip.

Clearly, the prisoners were hungry, thirsty, scared, and angry about the lies that Schmitt and Prauss had spread about their freedom. Guards in the train cars would most likely have prevented the Breendonk prisoners from talking, but with their eyes and with their gestures they would have been able to communicate their distress to each other. If they tried to peer out the side of the shade, they were hit in the head with a rifle butt.

Perhaps René Blieck, to pass the time, silently recited poetry to himself. Perhaps he even created new poems in his mind as the train traveled for two and a half days.

The train station at Neuengamme Concentration Camp, c. 1944.

The train finally stopped at Curslak, Germany. When the doors opened, twenty SS guards were standing on the platform to escort the prisoners to their destination: Neuengamme, a former brick factory near Hamburg that the Nazis had turned into a concentration camp.

As they entered the camp, which housed more than 6,300 prisoners at the time and about 105,000 over the course of the war, they passed a ten-foot-tall electrified barbed-wire fence. Nearby signs read WARNING—NEUTRAL ZONE—6000 VOLTS. They were ordered to the huge square where *Appell* was usually taken three times a day.

There, the SS began to inspect their belongings, confiscating any food so that it could be sent to the camp kitchen. The Breendonk prisoners had none, but the better-fed Huy prisoners had food parcels from their families. When the Breendonk prisoners realized this, they began to tear open the

Huy packages and stuff their mouths with food. Even jam from broken jars was scooped up from the ground, peppered with glass fragments, and eaten by the Breendonk prisoners, who cut themselves in the frenzy. In ten minutes, all the food was consumed.

Henderickx heard one of the SS guards tell another, "How is it possible that our colleagues stationed in Belgium have managed such a result? Their methods must certainly be more effective than ours."

Roll call at Neuengamme was depicted in this drawing by the former prisoner Hans Peter Sørensen.

Only Adrien Henderickx ever wrote about his experience on this transport. Of the 105 prisoners on the train, only twenty-one—including two of the ten Jews—would be alive when the war ended.

21.

A TEMPORARY LULL

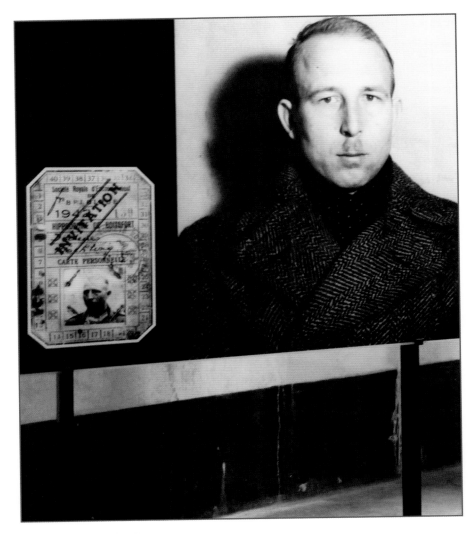

Dr. Hans Köchling.

The inspections at Breendonk brought its first year as a concentration camp to an end. The *Militärverwaltung* requested camp authorities to provide more food, to improve the medical care, and to clarify the rules for the internment and release of prisoners.

As a result, rations were increased, though they were still insufficient. In October, however, prisoners could once again receive food packages from their families. Some prisoners were so overwhelmed with this sudden influx of food that they could not eat it. One man, Paul Lévy recalled, received a beautiful pear in a package from home. He admired it, caressed it, and in the end could not eat the fruit; it spoiled. Others conserved their food insanely. One prisoner learned to cut his bread into fourteen minute slices so that he could eat some and squirrel the rest away. Another diced his bread into hundreds of tiny cubes, then ate them with a spoon, believing that he would have more to eat this way.

Perhaps the most surprising outcome was the decision to release some prisoners over the next few months, especially Jews whose only crime was returning to Belgium after trying to escape the German invasion.

In part because of these changes, for eight months after September 22 there were no more deaths at the camp.

In early October, Belgian radio, broadcasting from London, reported that the journalist Paul Lévy had died from abuse at Breendonk. Not long after, Lévy's wife was contacted by Mrs. Verdickt, who told her that although Lévy was quite ill, he was "not yet dead." The false report worried the German military administration, because Lévy was a well-known prisoner whose death or acknowledged suffering at Breendonk would be detrimental to the *Militärverwaltung*'s reputation. Perhaps because of this, he was soon admitted to the camp *Revier*.

*Paul Lévy,
by Jacques
Ochs.*

On November 20, as he drifted in and out of consciousness, he awoke to see a member of the SS at the foot of his
bed.

"Are you able to stand up?" the man asked. When
Lévy told him that he was, he ordered, "Out! Put on your
civilian clothes!"

Lévy retrieved his clothes from the storeroom, then went
to the office to formalize his release by signing the pledge to
remain silent about his experience at Breendonk.

He was forced to stand at the wall one more time, where
he was asked, "Do you understand? You will keep quiet now?"

Lévy nodded.

Before he left the camp that day, he had another encounter with Jürgen Jacobsohn, a man that Lévy judged to be bitter and desperate, two traits he detested. Still, various documents in Jacobsohn's immigration file suggest that he probably had good reasons for such feelings. Even before he was arrested and sent to Breendonk, he had become disillusioned with Germany and, perhaps in some ways, with Belgium.

A Jew, Jacobsohn had left Germany in 1933, after Adolf Hitler had become chancellor, to avoid persecution. In 1934, a year after he arrived in Belgium as a university student, an acquaintance went to the Brussels police to share her concern that Jacobsohn was a German spy. Nothing could have been further from the truth.

He was committed to the spread of Esperanto, an invented language that many hoped would bring the people of the world closer together. But Esperanto was viewed with great suspicion, by both the German and Belgium governments. Belgian police monitored his involvement with the organization and added reports to his immigration file when he attended conferences, including one entitled Youth for Peace. In 1935, shortly before he married his wife, he left school and became a self-employed electrician. Soon after, his mother and grandmother moved in with the newlyweds, and Jacobsohn quickly assumed responsibility for a family of four.

On September 1, 1939—the day that Hitler's troops invaded Poland to begin World War II—he wrote the Belgian government to ask for permission to become a naturalized citizen. He explained that he was an established business owner in a country that he now considered his permanent home. His request went unanswered. Eighteen months later he was arrested for unspecified reasons and sent to Breendonk, where he was repeatedly abused by *Zugführer* Obler and others.

And so on the day that Lévy left Breendonk, he heard Jacobsohn mutter, "The pig . . . the pig . . . there he goes . . . he's free."

Perhaps that is exactly what Jacobsohn said, still angry that Lévy had stolen a potato from him. Perhaps there were more reasons for his anger, including other contentious but unrecorded encounters between the two men. But no one will ever know what Jacobsohn truly thought, because he never wrote about his time at the camp; it is only Lévy's account of Jacobsohn that exists.

————

Lévy was released on the same day as Abraham Feldberg; both men went into hiding to avoid any further encounters with the SIPO-SD. A friend who saw Lévy soon after called him "a physical ruin." But Lévy managed to follow through on a promise to at least one prisoner. He contacted the parents of Ernest Landau in Vienna to tell them that their son was still alive.

Jürgen Jacobsohn identity card, 1934.

Eight days later, on November 28, Vladimir Lasareff, who had already spent months in a hospital in Antwerp as doctors worked to save his foot from amputation, was also released. And sometime between November 21 and 28, Jürgen Jacobsohn himself was freed. The actual date has been lost, but on November 29, a newly liberated Jacobsohn reported to the town hall in his Brussels suburb, where he renewed his ID card. The photograph on the document dramatically revealed how he had

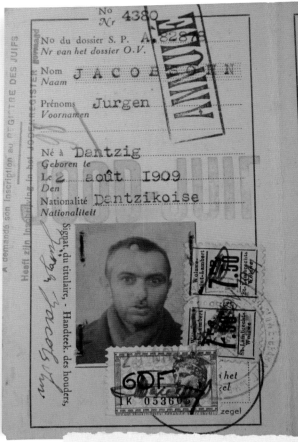

Jürgen Jacobsohn identity card, 1941.

been abused at Breendonk during his five months of captivity.

By December, only a handful of the original Room 1 prisoners from 1940 remained. Jacques Ochs was one, left behind in deteriorating health. His main symptoms of badly swollen ankles and fainting spells, signs that his body was breaking down, were most likely related to starvation edema.

Somehow managing to sidestep Prauss, Dr. Singer was able to admit Ochs to the *Revier*. Then he urged Dr. Köchling to help the artist. On December 26, 1941, after SS-Major Schmitt and SS-Lieutenant Prauss had gone home for lunch,

Dr. Köchling took Ochs to the hospital in Antwerp in his own car. There, Ochs had a bath, put on a pair of pajamas, and got into a real bed with clean sheets. He stayed for almost two months, eating regular meals, gaining weight, and recovering from the Hell of Breendonk.

On February 20, he was sufficiently improved to be returned to the camp. Back in Room 1, his few remaining friends were surprised to see him, since they had heard that he had been freed three weeks earlier. Figuring that his release was now imminent, they crowded around him and asked for favors once he was outside: send food packages, deliver messages to family, help them gain their own freedom.

Suddenly, they were interrupted by a shrill whistle.

A Flemish SS guard entered the room and told Ochs to follow him; he was going home. He was shaved by the barber, then handed his clothes by Herszel Frydman. Frydman's three sons had already been released in late January.

What concerned Ochs most was how he would take the thirty or so drawings he had made while at Breendonk. He asked the SS sergeant in charge of the storeroom if he could keep them. The sergeant said he would have to ask his superiors. He took the drawings into the next room to ask permission but returned without them. Ochs concluded that they had been confiscated. But when he unpacked his suitcase later, he found them hidden at the bottom. He had, he wrote, an "SS guardian angel."

Then he followed the SS guards down "the long tunnel at the end of which the light of freedom grew and grew and from behind, already muffled, the infernal noises of forced labor from this cursed place."

———

During the nine-month lull, almost no new prisoners were

registered, except for some who were scheduled to be transported to other concentration camps. By the end of June, only about 120 prisoners were interned at Breendonk, a marked contrast to the 450 or so men imprisoned there the previous summer.

SS-Major Schmitt was unhappy about the release of so many prisoners and requested a transfer to the *Waffen*–SS, the army of the *Schutzstaffel*. When he heard nothing, he may have wondered if his career had come to an end.

Instead, another opportunity was about to present itself.

A SECOND CAMP

July–August 1942

22.

THE *SAMMELLAGER* IN MECHELEN

Charlotte Hamburger.

O n July 15, 1942, SS-Major Philipp Schmitt received an additional assignment: he was ordered to open a *Sammellager*, or collection camp, from which the Jews of Belgium would be deported. The camp would be housed in the old Dossin army barracks in Mechelen, just a few miles east of Breendonk. Schmitt would be in charge of both camps.

Charlotte Hamburger, a Jewish woman whose family had emigrated from the Netherlands to Belgium in 1913, would be among the first arrivals and victims at this new camp.

———

Hamburger had married a Belgian man named Louis De Houwer, who had been raised a Catholic. The couple had a three-year-old daughter named Albertine. Neither set of grandparents was especially happy with the couple's interfaith marriage, but they all loved their granddaughter.

Hamburger and De Houwer, like the poet René Blieck, were members of the resistance group Independence Front. De Houwer reportedly collected arms and ammunition for resistance fighters and may have participated in a number of attacks. Hamburger delivered explosives and orders to various cells within the organization. It was dangerous work, but De Houwer and Hamburger performed it out of their love for Belgium.

On the morning of November 21, 1941, Charlotte took Albertine to visit her grandmother who lived in a suburb of Antwerp. During the visit, two agents from the SIPO-SD arrived at the house and asked to see Louis De Houwer. Realizing that he was in danger, Hamburger calmly told the agents that he was at work. As soon as they left, she telephoned Louis to warn that the SIPO-SD was on its way to his office. At that moment, he fled and went into hiding.

Albertine De Houwer (center of children) is pictured with her grandmother Esther Blom, the mother of Charlotte Hamburger.

The SIPO-SD agents were not amused that they had missed him, so they returned and arrested Charlotte. When her mother was taken from the house, Albertine cried and called for her. Her grandmother told the girl that her mother would return the next day. The truth was that Albertine would never see either of her parents again.

———

Before her arrest, the SIPO-SD did not know that Hamburger was Jewish. Soon after her imprisonment at the Begijnenstraat Prison in Antwerp, agents discovered her ancestry.

When the Germans invaded Belgium, they took great pains to assure Jews living in Belgium that they would remain safe under the *Militärverwaltung*. During the first eighteen months of its occupation, however, the military administration slowly began to enact a number of ordinances concerning Jews. On October 28, 1940, the first few were announced,

Begijnenstraat Prison, Antwerp.

including the condition that cafés and restaurants owned by Jews had to be labeled as "Jewish-owned businesses" with signs placed in the front windows. But the most important ordinance was to require all Jews in Belgium to sign the Jewish Register. Although her parents complied with this decree, Charlotte Hamburger chose not to, perhaps because she was married to a Christian or because she wanted to protest the decree. This may have added to her troubles in prison.

Charlotte Hamburger's mother completed the Jewish Register on December 13, 1940.

Seven months later, the next series of ordinances was announced. Now Jews had to declare all their property, cash, and securities; they could no longer work as civil servants or teachers; they had to turn in their radios. Three months later, at the end of August, a strict curfew between eight p.m. and seven a.m. was imposed on Jews.

All of these ordinances were in effect when Charlotte Hamburger was arrested in November 1941. Shortly afterward, others were enacted. Jewish children were no longer permitted to attend public schools. Jews in Belgium were no longer allowed to travel abroad. Unemployed Jews could be deported and forced to work for the Germans. On May 27,

The fabric printed with Stars of David that the Jews in Belgium were required to purchase.

1942, all Belgian Jews over the age of five were required to purchase and wear a yellow Star of David on their clothing. A small piece of fabric containing the outline of three stars was sold for one Belgian franc. Any Jew caught not wearing the yellow star "would receive a single punishment: Breendonk."

Even though she was incarcerated, Hamburger probably learned about each new ordinance, since reading material was permitted in regular prisons. But she had other things on her mind, which were reflected in the careful letters that she was occasionally permitted to write to her family.

She was concerned about her survival in prison and about gaining her release. She asked her parents to send her packages with items that she needed: soap, hair clips, mouthwash, toilet paper, shampoo, underwear, and a photograph of Albertine. She wrote instructions about her laundry, which had to be picked up by her family every Friday, because no laundry service was provided for prisoners. She mentioned to her parents that she wanted to make a dress for Albertine from one of her own dresses. She even made her daughter a doll out of her underclothes, stuffed it with straw from her mattress, and hid it in her bag of dirty laundry so that it could be smuggled out. When Albertine received the doll, she treasured it.

"Does she still remember her mommy," Charlotte wrote her parents at one point, "and do you often speak of me, would she still know me?"

But there was more that concerned Hamburger. When she was arrested, she was seven months pregnant, though she never mentioned this in her letters. More than anything else, she hoped that as the wife of a Belgian citizen, she would soon be released. But because she was a Jewish immigrant as well as a member of the resistance (and married to another in hiding), her release was unlikely.

What's more, the Nazis were designing something else for the Jews of Belgium and Europe. Charlotte Hamburger's life would soon be in the hands of SS-Major Schmitt.

———

During Hamburger's imprisonment, the Nazis drew up plans for the *Endlösung,* or "Final Solution," a Nazi euphemism for their decision to exterminate the Jews of Europe. In July 1942, Belgium's role, under the direction of the *Militärverwaltung,* was made clear: a *Sammellager* in Mechelen run by the SS was to be created. There, the Jews of Belgium would be collected and periodically transported by train to Auschwitz-Birkenau, where most would be immediately murdered in the gas chambers. The *Militärverwaltung* chose to spare the 4,000 Belgian citizens who were Jewish, at least at first, for fear of angering the public; instead they concentrated on arresting the 66,000 Jewish immigrants—predominantly from Poland, Austria, and Germany—who were living in the country.

The doll made by Charlotte Hamburger for Albertine. It is now displayed at the Kazerne Dossin Museum in Mechelen.

As one historian wrote, SS-*Sammellager* Mechelen was to become "the waiting room for Auschwitz." For approximately 210 Jews, Breendonk itself became the waiting room for the *Sammellager*. It made perfect sense to the SS, then, to select the commandant of Breendonk, SS-Major Philipp Schmitt, to run both camps. As with Breendonk, he was given almost no time to prepare it.

23

TRANSPORT II TO
AUSCHWITZ-BIRKENAU

Jews who responded to the Arbeitseinsatzbefehl *at the end of July 1942 and beginning of August were gathered in the courtyard of SS-Sammellager* Mechelen.

171

In anticipation of the opening of the *Sammellager* on July 27, the SS launched the first unofficial razzia—a "massive, organized, and sudden arrest" of Jewish immigrants who had not broken any of the anti-Jewish measures passed by the *Militärverwaltung*—on July 22 in Antwerp. At least 164 people, including some 100 women, were rounded up near Central Station. Fishel Horowitz had arranged to meet his wife, Rosa Reisla, who was arriving on the eleven o'clock train from Brussels; both were arrested and sent to Mechelen. Because the *Sammellager* was not yet open, they and the others were transferred to Breendonk.

Fishel Horowitz.

Rosa Reisla.

Aline Loitzanski.

Der Militärbefehlshaber
in Belgien und Nordfrankreich
- Militärverwaltungschef -
B. d. S. Abt. II

Brüssel, den ....

Arbeitseinsatzbefehl Nr.

Herrn/Frau/Fräulein

....

....

Mit sofortiger Wirkung gelangen Sie zum Arbeitseinsatz.
Sie haben sich daher
am ...., den .... 1942 bis .... Uhr in dem Sammellager
M e c h e l n, « Dossin-Kaserne », Lierschesteenweg, einzufinden.

Die Abreise ist so frühzeitig anzutreten, dass ein rechtzeitiges Eintreffen unter allen
Umständen gewährleistet ist.

An Ausrüstungsgegenständen sind mitzubringen :

1.) Verpflegung für 14 Tage (nur nichtverderbliche Lebensmittel wie Hülsenfrüchte, Grau-
pen, Haferflocken, Mehl, Konserven usw.)

2.) 1 Paar derbe Arbeitsstiefel, 2 Paar Socken, 2 Hemden, 2 Unterhosen, 1 Arbeitsanzug
bezw. Kleid, 2 Wolldecken, 2 Garnituren Bettzeug, Essnapf, Trinkbecher, 1 Löffel,
1 Pullover.

3.) Lebensmittel -und Kleiderkarten, Identitätskarte und sonstige Ausweispapiere.

Im übrigen haben Sie den Anweisungen des Beauftragten der Vereinigung der Juden
in Belgien unbedingt Folge zu leisten.

Es wird Ihnen ausdrücklich untersagt, bei irgendwelchen deutschen oder belgischen
Behörden oder Einzelpersonen Einspruch gegen diesen Befehl zu erhaben. Etwaige Ein-
wendungen können im Sammellager vorgebracht werden. Falls Sie sich im Sammellager
nicht zu dem vorgeschriebenen Zeitpunkt melden, erfolgt Ihre Festnahme und Verbrin-
gung in ein Konzentrationslager nach Deutschland und die Einziehung Ihres gesamten
Vermögens.

Diese Aufforderung ist beim Eintreffen im Sammellager abzugeben.

Im Auftrage :

The Arbeitseinsatzbefehl *instructed recipients to arrive at* SS-Sammellager
Mechelen on a specific day and time so that they could be deployed for work.

The next day, Israel Rosengarten was arrested with some
seven others on the Brussels-Antwerp train, when SIPO-SD
officers stormed through the carriages looking for Jews. Some
were able to take off their yellow stars and escape, but eight
were trapped and sent to Breendonk. The following day, Aline
Loitzanski was arrested and taken to Breendonk, where she

was allowed to write a letter to her family requesting personal items such as soap.

In all, about 210 Jews were detained in late July and imprisoned at Breendonk. Because this was a temporary placement, however, most were never registered at the camp.

———

Once the *Sammellager* was ready, the SIPO-SD employed a less aggressive approach in gathering Jews. Between July 25 and September 3, 1942, a letter was sent to some 12,000 Jewish immigrants in Belgium. This *Arbeitseinsatzbefehl*, or work deployment order, required the recipient to report to the *Sammellager* on a certain day at a certain time so that the person could be sent east to work. Even older schoolchildren received the work order. Authorities took great pains to stress that this was "a work order and not a deportation order."

The letter warned the recipient that he or she was "expressly forbidden to revolt against this order by contacting any German or Belgian authorities. . . . Any objections can be raised at the *Sammellager*. Failure to report . . . at the assigned time will lead to arrest and deportation to a concentration camp in Germany, and the sequestration of all your property." Of course, taking possession of the Jews' property was a second but quite important goal of the SIPO-SD.

Because the letter clearly told the recipient how to prepare for work, many believed that this was a legitimate request. Precise instructions listed exactly what the person should bring: identity and ration cards, fourteen days' worth of food, a pair of heavy-duty work boots, two pairs of socks and underwear, and household items that included two sets of sheets, a bowl, and a spoon.

As a result of the letter, 4,023 Jews voluntarily came to the camp during the first five weeks, but this was far fewer than the 10,000 that the SIPO-SD had hoped for.

Other Jews who were already incarcerated, such as Charlotte Hamburger, were transferred to the *Sammellager* from their prison cells. By that time in early August, Hamburger would have given birth, although the fate of her child remains a mystery. Was her baby healthy at birth? Was it stillborn? Was it taken from her and secretly given to another family to raise? Was it killed by her jailers? Whatever happened, the infant was not with her when she arrived in Mechelen.

A few days later, the first transport of a thousand Jews left on August 4, 1942. On board were five former Breendonk prisoners as well as Rajzla Bicher, the wife of Mozes Louft, prisoner number 59, who had been shot at Breendonk a month earlier. Bicher arrived soon after the *Sammellager* had opened, with the work-order letter in hand. Did she know that her husband had been murdered at Breendonk? Was she hoping to save herself from the same fate by voluntarily accepting the work order? There is no way to know.

An example of the placard that prisoners were forced to wear while awaiting deportation on a transport.

At first, Hamburger was in a hopeful mood, as reflected in the first of two postcards, mailed on August 7, to her family:

> Dear Mama, Dad, and my little treasure,
> I'm writing you again. Why don't I hear anything from you, and where is the package with clothes? Send also some bread, jam, eggs, a piece of sausage. I'm still trying to get home. Since I am married anyway to an Aryan, they say I don't have to go away. We will see, keep good courage. Be good to my little treasure. I think about you so often. Send a lot of clothes and towels, soap.

The second postcard, written the next day, had a much different tone. By then, she had probably learned that she was scheduled for the next transport. When the list for a transport was drawn up, every selected prisoner was given a cardboard sign to wear around her neck showing the details of her impending deportation.

Hamburger was now desperate for help:

The last postcard that Charlotte Hamburger wrote was postmarked August 9–10, 1942.

Dear Mama, Grandmother, Dad and all. Please send me by return express post, my marriage certificate or extract of marriage, at the Town Hall, and a copy of birth certificate, then I may go home. Quickly please *. . . Bring it by train and hand it over.* My marriage certificate is most likely with Mama. Kisses for the child. Birth certificate is also in the town hall.

Nachman Feltscher.

Whether she ever heard from her family—whether they were able to bring the documents she requested—is not known. Even with the documents, however, the SS would still have transported her.

Three days later, she was placed on Transport II. On it were 460 men, 488 women, and 51 children, ranging in age from five to sixty-three. Two Breendonk prisoners had also been assigned to the transport: Nachman Feltscher (prisoner number 64) and Mozes Weissbart (prisoner number 45). Not much is known about either man except that Feltscher was a hairdresser and Weissbart was a leather goods dealer and that both had fled Nazi oppression, Feltscher from Austria, Weissbart from Germany.

Weissbart had written to the Belgian justice minister in 1939 soon after he had arrived from Munich, Germany, without a passport or visa. In the letter, he requested political asylum for a simple reason: "Having been persecuted by the Gestapo, I was forced to flee so that I would not be placed in a concentration

Mozes Weissbart, 1940.

camp." He wanted to stay in Belgium long enough to make arrangements to move to the United States. Instead he was arrested and sent to Breendonk. Although the records are not complete, he may have been released around the time that he received a work-order letter. He voluntarily went to the *Sammellager,* perhaps preferring that alternative to imprisonment at Breendonk, and was placed on Transport II.

Like everyone else on the train, Charlotte Hamburger had been told that she was being sent to a labor camp. The train was composed of third-class passenger carriages that contained small windowed compartments crammed with prisoners on two facing wooden benches. Each carriage had a series of these compartments, separate and unconnected from the others, reached by its own small door to the platform at the station. Armed guards would have been stationed on the roofs of the cars, but that did not stop some passengers from jumping from the train, trying to escape.

For the first nineteen transports to Auschwitz-Birkenau, the SS used third-class rail cars like this to carry the prisoners.

All that remains of Bunker 2 (or the "red house") at Auschwitz-Birkenau is its foundations. Prisoners would have been instructed to undress in barracks, the foundation of which is visible in the background on the left.

Transport II traveled some 720 miles and arrived in Auschwitz, Poland, on August 13 at a time of day that is no longer known. In August 1942, the arrival platform was a mile and a half from their intended destination of Auschwitz-Birkenau. Also called Auschwitz II, this new subcamp of Auschwitz was still under construction. Eventually, it would house 200,000 prisoners, making it the largest Nazi concentration camp. It would also become the most infamous death camp, where more than 1.3 million people (including almost 1.1 million Jews) were murdered, most in the gas chambers.

A selection took place at the unloading ramp: 518 prisoners (290 men and 228 women) were separated from the others and, without a word of explanation, sent off to be deloused, registered, and assigned to work in the camp. The 481 others,

Today a small memorial indicates the location of Bunker 1.

including all 51 children, were sent to be gassed. Because no documents exist showing that Hamburger was registered and tattooed as a prisoner, she may well have been sent to the gas chamber immediately. However, when the camp was evacuated in January 1945, the SS burned many of the original documents; her registration may have been among those destroyed. All that can be said with certainty is that she was transported to Auschwitz-Birkenau; from that point, there is no record of her existence.

If she was selected for the gas chamber and the transport arrived at night, trucks would have taken Hamburger and the other prisoners to the vicinity of the gas chamber at Auschwitz-Birkenau. If the train arrived during the day, the condemned prisoners would have been marched to the camp; only those who could not walk were given a ride. As they did, a car marked with the symbol of the Red Cross would have followed the prisoners; Hamburger and the others would have been unaware that the car was a ruse and had nothing to do with the Red Cross. Instead, it contained the deadly Zyklon B gas pellets that would be used to kill them. In the car as well was "an SS doctor with medicines and an oxygen bottle for use in an emergency, such as the accidental poisoning of SS men taking part in the gassing."

In August 1942, only two gas chambers—both old farmhouses that had been converted by the SS—existed at

Auschwitz-Birkenau. The first, called Bunker 1 by the SS or the "red house" by Auschwitz prisoners, could hold 800 people in two rooms. The second, called Bunker 2 or the "white house," could fit 1,200 people into four rooms. It is not known to which gas chamber the Jews from Transport II were sent.

At one of the bunkers, the prisoners would have been told to undress either in a nearby barrack or behind some hedges. As they were herded naked inside, they might have noticed a sign that read *Zum Baden* (To the Baths). On the exit door, another sign read *Zur Desinfektion* (To the Disinfection Area). Next, the door was quickly closed and locked. Then Zyklon B gas pellets were dropped into each room through openings in the outer walls. Although the people died within a few minutes, the SS waited a half hour to open the door. Then an SS doctor verified that the victims were dead before ordering a team of prisoners, members of the *Sonderkommando,* to drag the corpses to a nearby pit, where they were burned to ash.

Perhaps, however, Charlotte Hamburger was selected for work. In that case, she would have lived, but only a little longer. Within the first week, thirteen working prisoners from Transport II died. By the end of the next week, a total of sixty had died. By the end of seven weeks, 155 of the 518 selected for work had perished. Existing documents do not indicate the causes of death, whether disease, starvation, beatings, suicide, or execution. No matter which it was, the overarching reason for the deaths was the Nazis' idea of extermination through work. Being selected for work was nothing short of murder for many prisoners at Auschwitz.

Only three of the 999 people on Transport II survived to the end of the war.

———

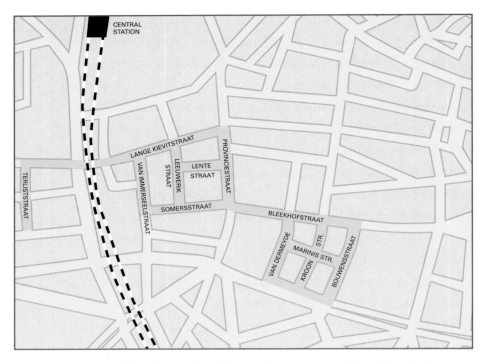

CENTRAL
STATION

TERLISTSTRAAT

LANGE KIEVITSTRAAT

VAN IMMERSEELSTRAAT

STRAAT

LEEUWERIK

LENTE
STRAAT

PROVINCIESTRAAT

SOMERSSTRAAT

BLEEKHOFSTRAAT

VAN DERMEYDE

MARINIS STR.

KROON

STR.

BOUWENSSTRAAT

This map of the first razzia in Antwerp, held on August 15–16, 1942, shows the streets that were blocked by the SS. About 845 Jews were arrested as a result of the house-to-house raids.

On August 15, the same day that 481 people from Transport II were murdered, the SIPO-SD began to enact a series of five large, well-planned razzias, intended to round up a large number of Jewish immigrants for other transports to Auschwitz-Birkenau. Four of the five razzias were held in Antwerp; the fifth was in Brussels.

Although Antwerp and Brussels were the two largest centers for Jews in Belgium, the razzias in Antwerp were much more effective. There, most Jews lived in neighborhoods directly around Central Station, which made it easier for the SIPO-SD to close off entire streets and go door to door in search of Jewish families. Further, local government officials and the Antwerp police were much more eager to comply with anti-Jewish ordinances to show their support for Nazi policies.

In Brussels, where local officials refused to cooperate with the *Militärverwaltung* and sell the yellow Stars of David to Jews, the Jewish population was spread out across the city, making large-scale roundups more difficult.

The first razzia took place in Antwerp on the evening of August 15 and early morning of August 16—just hours after the Jewish Sabbath ended—when the SIPO-SD arrested 845 Jews, ranging from three-month-old Simon Lic to eighty-eight-year-old Henri Rappaport. These arrests provided the bulk of the prisoners for Transport IV.

On August 28 and 29, another 943 Jews were arrested in the next Antwerp razzia. This time the Antwerp police acted alone, without the help of the SIPO-SD. Some Jews quickly wrote letters that they left behind; Boris Averbuch wrote, "It is five o'clock in the morning. They have come to take us from our beds. I do not know to where or to what. Farewell." When

Some Jews from Transport VIII were abused and photographed by the SS before their deportation.

other Jews in the cordoned-off area realized that only the Antwerp police were looking for them, they began to resist, hiding wherever they could to avoid being detected. In their official report afterward, the Antwerp police "displayed a clear conscience in what they had done and even referred to 'the ill will of the Jewish inhabitants'" who refused to cooperate with their arrest.

The final three razzias took place in September. On September 3 and 4 around two of Brussels's main train stations, 660 Jews were arrested and included on Transport VIII to Auschwitz-Birkenau. On September 11 and 12, which was also Rosh Hashanah, or the Jewish New Year, a daylight raid was carried out in Antwerp. More of a random hunt, in which SIPO-SD agents stopped anyone suspected of being a Jew on the street and asked for identity papers, it resulted in the

SS-Major Philipp Schmitt poses at SS-Sammellager Mechelen with his automobile.

arrest of 681 Jews. With these victims, the SIPO-SD was able to fill Transport IX and X. Finally, a three-day razzia in Antwerp that began September 22 produced 761 arrests intended for Transport XI.

———————

In all, between August 4, 1942, and July 31, 1944, there were twenty-seven transports that took 25,031 Jews to Auschwitz from SS-*Sammellager* Mechelen; most were sent directly to the gas chamber, and only 1,217 survived.

Of course, SS-Major Schmitt continued transports as well from Breendonk, intended primarily for non-Jewish political prisoners. After the first deportation of Breendonk prisoners in September 1941, the next four occurred between May and November 1942, when a total of 393 prisoners were sent to Mauthausen, a concentration camp in Austria.

Others would follow.

CAMP OF TERROR

September 1942–April 1944

24

THE POSTAL WORKERS
OF BRUSSELS

The central post office in Brussels, c. 1945.

D uring the first two years of *Auffanglager* Breendonk, its prisoners were mostly Jews, communists, and ordinary criminals. As increased acts of sabotage rattled the *Militärverwaltung,* the SIPO-SD expanded its roundups of so-called terrorists and resistance fighters. These prisoners changed the face of Breendonk. Among the first to be singled out in this new crackdown was a special group of forty postal workers from Brussels, who were arrested in the early morning hours of September 1.

Désiré Piens, one of the workers, found two SIPO-SD agents and a policeman at his front door; one pointed a gun inches from his face. While he and his wife were questioned, his house was ransacked: the bed overturned, cabinets emptied, floorboards ripped up, and furniture moved. Even the toilet was checked for incriminating evidence.

Désiré Piens.

Some of the arrested workers were supervisors, but most were ordinary letter carriers. They had resisted the German occupation by delivering underground newspapers on their routes, holding back letters addressed to the SIPO-SD or *Militärverwaltung* offices, and daring to go on strike, not once but twice—with a third strike threatened.

They had also interfered with censorship of the mail. When a German censor discovered mail that he wanted to examine at the central post office in Brussels, the letters were secured in a locked office to await inspection. Some postal workers, however, had a duplicate key to the office. Before the German inspector could arrive, they would replace the letters with harmless ones. Other employees had also made a copy of a rubber stamp, which read *GEPRÜFT* (inspected), used by the censor to indicate that

This typical flyer printed by the Independence Front encouraged Belgians to help Hitler send his troops over the cliff and into the precipice.

a letter had been examined. This way, the postal workers could "sabotage the censor."

———

By eight o'clock on the morning of September 1, the forty postal workers had been assembled at the SIPO-SD office in Brussels to confirm their identities. By nine, the men had been taken to Breendonk. By ten, they were at work outside. When it was lunchtime, they were sent to their barrack for soup. Désiré Piens looked into the large container of foul-smelling liquid and observed some wilted cabbage leaves floating on top, and a few potatoes. Almost none of the postmen could eat it even though they hadn't had any food all day.

It would not be long, Piens admitted later, before they would give anything for an extra spoonful of the same soup— or a few potato peels rescued from the garbage. Only a week after they arrived at Breendonk, food packages were prohibited once again, and signs of starvation edema—the illness that had afflicted many prisoners during the summer of 1941—began to reappear.

In October, forty-four cases of starvation edema were diagnosed; in November, there were eighty-six. This sudden surge in extreme malnutrition caused the *Militärverwaltung* to request an increased bread ration. Even the new camp physician, Dr. Heinz Pohl, stated that unless rations were augmented, there would be more deaths. But the bread ration was not increased, and 101 out of the 240 prisoners at the camp were diagnosed with the life-threatening condition at the beginning of December 1942.

Piens saw what happened to a healthy group of some ninety men who were transferred to Breendonk from another prison in northern France. These prisoners from Douai had been well fed at their former prison; they had also been able to supplement their diet with food parcels from their families. Piens and the other prisoners at Breendonk marveled at their robust physical condition: the Douai prisoners were not especially tall, but they were solidly built and probably weighed an average of about 200 pounds, according to Piens's estimate. The Breendonk *Arbeitsführers* were ecstatic when they saw these men, because they could assign them the hardest jobs at the work site and know that they would perform well.

Like every other prisoner, however, the Douai prisoners were fed the Breendonk diet. Fifteen days later, they had each lost substantial weight, which robbed them of their strength. As Piens explained after the war, eventually "the lack of food takes its toll: your strength fades, your activity suffers, and as your work capacity declines every day, you increasingly expose yourself to suffer abuse from your torturers who claimed that the inmates are fed too well."

And there were new, very eager torturers at Breendonk: the Flemish SS and a new *Zugführer*.

———

After the inspections were completed in September 1941, the SIPO-SD replaced the *Wehrmacht* soldiers with Flemish SS

Belgians were encouraged to join the Waffen-SS, *the military force of the Nazis.*

guards. Six were sent to the camp in September 1941, in part to take over the supervision of the work site and the barracks. By the time Breendonk was evacuated three years later, a total of nineteen Flemish SS had been assigned to the camp, though never more than ten concurrently. None had signed up to join the Flemish SS with the intention of working at an *Auffanglager*. Most had been unemployed and enlisted in the *Waffen*-SS to receive a paycheck. After training, however, they were considered unfit for or unwilling to perform military service at the front lines, and the SIPO-SD determined that they would better serve as guards at Breendonk. Most held the lowest rank, but they were anxious to become part of the new Nazi order in Belgium.

If these men hoped to earn respect from the SS itself, they were mistaken. SS-Lieutenant Prauss berated them. To him, the Flemish SS were not authentically German. If they erred in some way, Prauss humiliated them in front of the prisoners. To the prisoners, these Belgian men were unpatriotic traitors who had chosen to collaborate with the German occupier.

Among them were Fernand Wyss and Richard De Bodt, who became the new terrors of Breendonk, often working as a team in abusing and murdering prisoners. After he learned that he would be stationed at Breendonk, Wyss told a friend, "I will teach the Jews how to work. If they don't listen to me, I will kill them." At Breendonk, Wyss became known for repeatedly greeting new prisoners with the warning, "This is Hell, and I am the Devil."

The Flemish SS guards Fernand Wyss (top) and Richard De Bodt (bottom) were assigned to Breendonk, where they terrorized the prisoners.

The prisoner Eduard Franckx recalled his arrival at the camp: Before he was registered, Wyss and De Bodt beat him and then demanded his two rings. He could remove the first ring without a problem, but when he had difficulty with his wedding ring, Wyss pulled out his knife and threatened, "Your finger or your ring." Then, as he began to slice Franckx's finger, the ring slipped off.

Zugführer Obler often assisted them in terrorizing prisoners, but Wyss and De Bodt also had another helper: a new *Zugführer* named Valère De Vos. De Vos was in charge of Room 10, which at least one prisoner

called "Breendonk within Breendonk," a description of the
even stricter discipline that De Vos administered there.
Once a communist, De Vos had traveled to Spain in 1936 to
fight in the Spanish civil war. Returning to Belgium bitter and
disillusioned, with crippling injuries from a gunshot wound to
the spine, De Vos had turned against communism by the start
of World War II, but that did not stop the SIPO-SD from arresting
him in July 1941, most likely because of his communist past.
At Breendonk, he was placed in a barrack with other devoted
communists. When he was finally appointed *Zugführer*, he
was ready to unleash his anger in league with Wyss, De Bodt,
and Obler.

———

Although only one prisoner had died between September
1941 and September 1942, that was about to change. Beginning
in October, seven prisoners, all Jews, died within a month.
One, Isaak Trost, was killed on October 30. Trost and two other
prisoners had been selected by the Flemish SS De Bodt to
help move his furniture and belongings to a new house in
Willebroek. Around noon, Trost saw his chance to escape and
jumped a wall. When he was discovered later in a nearby
turnip field, De Bodt punched him in the stomach so hard that
Trost doubled over and fell on top of a manure pile. Then De
Bodt grabbed a bayonet and stabbed him in the abdomen,
while a guard bayoneted his chest. Finally, De Bodt shot him to
death.

The one civilian witness to the murder was a Mrs.
Dalemans. "There was no reason whatsoever," she told the
police in November 1944, two months after Belgium was
liberated, "for killing this person . . . after he had been taken
prisoner. Whilst they were inflicting him with bayonet wounds,
I saw him trying to ward them off and it seemed to me that he
implored them not to ill-treat him any further. He pressed one

hand against his side and the other he raised above his head in a token of submission."

The body of Isaak Trost, like that of Mozes Louft, was displayed in the courtyard, and prisoners were forced to walk past.

———————

From mid-November to mid-January, fourteen others—all non-Jews—died. Five were postmen. The deaths of two of them were described by other prisoners.

Jean Van Boven.

One day, Jean Van Boven collapsed on the work site. The forty-four-year-old postman had been deprived of food, beaten at random, and forced to work beyond his ability. When his body gave out on the dismal, rainy morning of November 20, De Bodt attacked him. Concealing a metal object in his fist, he grabbed Van Boven's collar, pulled him up from the ground, then punched him hard between the eyes. When De Bodt released him, Van Boven slumped down in the mud, where he lay unconscious in the pouring rain for the rest of the day. No one was allowed to help him. Only when the workday was over were prisoners ordered to take Van Boven in a wheelbarrow to the *Revier.* He died there without regaining consciousness.

Sebastien De Greef

Sebastien De Greef was singled out by *Zugführer* De Vos. Assigned to wheelbarrow duty, the fifty-five-year-old man could not keep up the pace.

"I will teach you to work," De Vos told De Greef, and repeatedly beat him with a truncheon, not once but three times during one hour.

On his knees after the third beating, De Greef pleaded with De Vos to kill him and end his misery.

De Vos replied, "A bullet costs too much money for you; my fists cost nothing." Then he pointed to the skull on the hat of his SS uniform. "This is what you will be in a while."

De Greef died on December 18, 1942.

In a report about the deaths of the five postmen in December, the highest-ranking German military doctor in occupied Belgium noted that De Greef had "died of lung infection, heart weakness, undernourishment" and starvation edema. No mention was made of the terrible beatings he had received from De Vos.

The postal worker François Vanderveken, before his imprisonment at Breendonk.

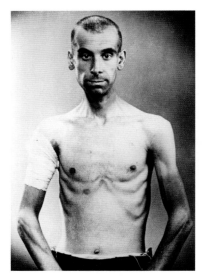

François Vanderveken, after his imprisonment.

Almost all the remaining postmen were released from Breendonk by July 1943, but they were hardly unscathed by their stay. Their physical decline could be clearly documented, for on their second day at the camp, they were given a health inspection. This new requirement, enacted in August 1942, meant that their weight on arrival at the camp had to be recorded. When the postman Jules Gysermans was released on January 26, 1943, after less than five months at Breendonk, he had lost fifty pounds. To demonstrate the extent of their suffering at Breendonk, he and some of the other postmen posed for photos.

The Hell of Breendonk was never more visible.

The postal worker Victor Van Hamme, before his imprisonment at Breendonk.

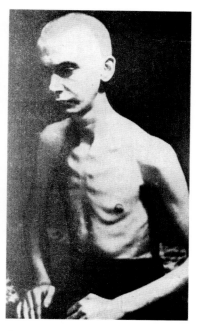

Victor Van Hamme, after his imprisonment.

25

THE FIRST
EXECUTIONS

Some Belgian resistance groups attacked railway lines to stop the flow of armaments and troops.

As the Belgian resistance movement carried out more sabotage against German troops and crucial infrastructure such as administrative offices, railway bridges, and power lines, the *Militärverwaltung* arrested more hostages and threatened to execute them after any new attack. But the executions were never carried out, because German officials believed that such reprisals might actually provoke the resistance further.

In November 1942, however, the assassination of a pro-Nazi Belgian politician forced the military administration to follow through on its threat. One of the first people to be affected by the decision was Louis De Houwer, the husband of Charlotte Hamburger.

Louis De Houwer.

Since November 1941, when his wife had called to warn him that the SIPO-SD had come to arrest him, De Houwer had hidden in a series of houses under a false name. Turned in by an informant, he was arrested on September 25 and taken to the same Antwerp prison as his wife. By that time he would have learned from his father that his wife had been sent first to SS-*Sammellager* Mechelen and then to a work camp. He probably would not have known that she had been transported to Auschwitz-Birkenau.

During his imprisonment at the Begijnenstraat Prison, he was able to write two letters to his parents. On October 10, aware that little Albertine's fourth birthday was approaching, he asked them what they were buying his daughter as a present. "Let me know in your next letter. In my thoughts I see her playing, romping about and talking. . . . She is becoming a real lady."

On October 25, he wrote again, expressing surprise that

they had not replied. "Soon it will be All Saints' Day, the day of the pancakes. Do you remember the splendid meals we have had . . . ? Those times will come again. . . ." Next, he asked for shoelaces and some gray yarn, because the "sweater you sent me has a hole in the elbow and I would like to fix it before it gets bigger." In closing, he asked his parents to tell Albertine "that her dad will come to play with her shortly and that she has to be good in the meantime, that he will talk to Santa Claus and that at Christmas, he will make a beautiful Christmas tree."

Soon after that, on a date that is no longer known, De Houwer was transferred to Breendonk, and his letters stopped.

———

No documents indicate how De Houwer spent his first weeks at Breendonk. Was he sent to work outside, or was he locked in a solitary-confinement cell? Was he deprived of food or beaten—or both? As a member of the resistance, he would have been a special target of the SS guards.

No matter how his time was spent, everything changed on November 19, 1942, when Jean Teughels, the Rexist mayor

Jean Teughels, mayor of Charleroi.

of Charleroi, a town in southern Belgium, was assassinated by unknown assailants who fled without being apprehended.

This attack was considered so serious that the military administration issued a stern warning to the Belgian public three days later: If the men responsible for the murder did not come forward by midnight on November 25, ten hostages considered to be communist terrorists would be shot. When the deadline passed without any suspects, the *Militärverwaltung* began to plan the execution of ten prisoners: eight at Breendonk and two others elsewhere.

This time they did not waver.

The funeral of Jean Teughels.

At Breendonk on the morning of November 27, Jozef Suy and a few other prisoners were assigned to erect ten wooden posts on the southeast side of the fort. This would become the execution place at Breendonk. As they dug the holes and placed the poles into the ground, Suy stood in front of one and joked, "Just the right size for me!"

Jozef Suy.

By two thirty that afternoon, Suy and the others had finished their work and were resting in their barrack when a guard entered and shouted four prisoner numbers. One was Suy's. The guard then proceeded to other barracks until the numbers of eight men had been announced. These were the men selected for execution at three p.m. that day. One of the eight was Louis De Houwer.

The condemned men from Breendonk had all arrived at the camp within the last three months. Some had already been

The execution ground at Breendonk.

designated as hostages or, like De Houwer, were members of a resistance group. Only one, Maurice Pierko, had been arrested for failing to comply with an order for compulsory labor in Germany. Some of the men, such as Joseph Bolanger, had been turned into the police by neighbors or acquaintances; when Bolanger's home was searched, the police found a cache of hidden weapons. At least three of these hostages—and possibly more—had been kept in solitary-confinement cells and beaten by the guards.

———

In the half hour that the eight men had to live, they would have been allowed to write a final letter to a family member, though it was unlikely to be delivered. They would have been given a small meal. They would have been allowed to have a final cigarette if they smoked. Jozef Suy, a nonsmoker, reportedly yelled, "Give me a cigar!" after his number was announced.

Just before three o'clock, they would have been

marched to the execution ground. There, the men would have been told to remove their shirt and jacket, and they would have been tied to the posts. Their bare chests would have been marked to help the *Wehrmacht* soldiers, who would now become the executioners, take better aim. Thirty-two soldiers would have been part of the firing squad, four firing at each condemned prisoner.

At three o'clock, the prisoners inside the fort fell silent after they heard multiple rifle bursts outside. Louis De Houwer's daughter, Albertine, had now lost both of her parents, under the command of SS-Major Schmitt.

The wedding photograph of Charlotte Hamburger and Louis De Houwer.

The next day, the *Militärverwaltung* publicized the executions in an attempt to demoralize any Belgians who hoped to sabotage the German occupier, but this attempt would not be successful. If anything, the deaths only propelled the resistance movement to take further action.

26.

THE *ARRESTANTEN*

Entrance to a solitary-confinement cell.

By the end of 1942, a new type of prisoner began to arrive in increasing numbers: the *Arrestant,* a person suspected of being an active member of the resistance who might possess valuable information about other anti-Nazi terrorists and their activities. The *Arrestanten* were isolated from the *Häftlingen,* or regular prisoners, and placed initially in solitary-confinement cells rather than barracks.

At first, the camp administration used the six solitary-confinement cells to the left of the entrance tunnel, where the *Häftlingen* were punished, or seven cagelike cells that were added a while later in the front-right gatehouse. However, the *Militärverwaltung* inspection in September 1941 found these two groups of cells more suitable for animals than humans. So thirty-two additional solitary-confinement cells, each less than twenty-five square feet, were built by converting barrack rooms 8 and 9.

———

The *Arrestanten* were not permitted to interact with either the *Häftlingen* or other *Arrestanten*. Every morning, they were awakened about six o'clock and eventually fed in their individual cells. By nine o'clock, each *Arrestant* had made the first of two daily trips to the courtyard toilet; otherwise, the only toilet was a small unlidded white enamel bucket in the cell.

The procedure for visiting the toilet was precise. When the SS guard unlocked his cell, an *Arrestant* was required to say, "Mr. SS Guard, this prisoner respectfully requests a bag." The guard then retrieved a heavy blue cloth bag from a hook at the end of the corridor and placed it completely over the prisoner's head before leading him away "like a dog on his leash." This hood prevented any communication with other prisoners and kept the *Arrestant* isolated, disoriented, and unidentified. Some *Arrestanten* were handcuffed to prevent escape; a few even had an iron ball attached by a chain to their

An Arrestant *would have to place the cloth bag over his head whenever he was escorted from his cell.*

ankles. If an *Arrestant* was caught attempting to remove or even adjust the bag to glimpse his surroundings, he was punished with a severe blow of a truncheon or rifle butt.

The trip to the toilets was humiliating.

"Do you want to piss or shit?" the guard would ask.

If the *Arrestant* had to urinate, he was taken to the communal urinal outside the toilet block. The guard then ordered, "Place your right hand on the buttons of your fly, open your fly . . . piss."

Only when he was back in his cell could he remove the cloth bag from his head.

The remainder of the day could seem interminable, broken up only by two more insubstantial meals and a second hooded visit to the toilet. At night, the *Arrestant* was allowed to curl up, still fully dressed, on the wooden bench to sleep.

An Arrestant *and his guards, by Jacques Ochs.*

If there was any benefit to being confined in the solitary cell, it was that the *Arrestanten* could avoid the forced labor on the work site. When Benoit Michiels was taken from his solitary cell after 100 days and sent to the work site, what he saw was a terrible shock. The prisoners, he observed, were "walking skeletons . . . [and] worked as though they were in a crazed nightmare. Terror reigned supreme. . . . I almost missed my detention cell. 'Men' hit their fellow creatures brutally, mercilessly. Wyss and De Bodt went from one to another and hit, hit them."

———

One prisoner well acquainted with the solitary-confinement cells was Jose Cornet, a painter at an auto-body shop, who

To pass the time, some prisoners surreptitiously carved drawings into the walls.

was arrested by the SIPO-SD for his work in writing underground newspapers for the resistance.

When he arrived at Breendonk, the guards shoved his
face into the wall of the tunnel six or seven times, dislocat-
ing his jaw. Then SS-Lieutenant Prauss knocked Cornet to the
ground and kicked him.

When he was finally able to stand up, Prauss asked him
one question: "Are you a communist?"

Hoping to avoid another beating, Cornet decided it was
better to tell the truth and say yes. But the word had barely
left his mouth when Prauss punched him in the face so hard that
he was propelled two feet away. He lost his balance and
fell sprawling. In the process, however, his jaw snapped back
into place.

Then Cornet was taken to solitary-confinement cell number 18, where he was given a slop bucket, a well-worn blanket,

and a scrap of used towel. He was told that it was forbidden to sit down or lean against the walls of the cell during the day or to talk to other *Arrestanten* at any time. He quickly became accustomed to his new routine.

Every morning, his acorn coffee was pushed through the slot in his door. A little later, he was permitted to go to the courtyard toilet, carrying his "jam jar" to empty. Once the cloth bag was placed over his head, he had to rely on the directions that were yelled by the accompanying guard. Some guards would yell *Links!* (or "left") when they knew he had to turn right, causing him to walk into a wall. If he spilled his bucket of waste, he had to clean it with his bare hands.

When he returned to his cell after the toilet, he was free until lunch, but free to do what? He began to walk. He found that he could take three steps from the door to the back wall,

Jose Cornet was able to project his voice through the bars and barbed wire across the top of his cell to speak to a prisoner in the cell opposite his.

turn around, and take three more. So he began to pace his cell as a way to entertain himself and relieve boredom.

As he walked, he let his imagination roam. Sometimes he tried to figure how many steps it would take to walk from his childhood home to the school he had attended. Other times, he invented complex multiplication problems to solve. He was surprised to find that the time passed quickly that way.

At night, he discovered that he could talk to the prisoner in the cell opposite his. If the two men leaned against the back wall of their respective cells and looked up, their voices would carry around the curve of the ceiling arch to the other side of the room. His new friend in the opposite cell, he learned, was Jean.

Even a small detail could bring him comfort. One morning when he was at the courtyard toilet, he heard a bird chirping. He had not seen the sky or breathed fresh air since he arrived at the camp. Hoping that his guard was momentarily distracted, he lifted the corner of his cloth bag. He glimpsed the bird pecking and chirping nearby. The sight was thrilling, despite his despair at being imprisoned.

That night, after he told Jean about his encounter with the bird, the other man asked, "What color was it?"

Cornet was dismayed when he realized that he did not remember. He had been so enthralled by the experience that he hadn't paid attention to every detail.

———————

One day, after the morning trip to the toilet, the guard pushed him inside the cell next door—number 20 instead of number 18. Cornet assumed that the guard must have made a mistake, but soon another man was placed in the cell with him.

His new roommate was an older man, Cornet surmised, who had been at Breendonk a long time. The man seemed to be in a trance, unaware that he now shared a cell with another

Prisoners placed in solitary-confinement cells often received half the food regular prisoners were allotted.

man. He spent the morning sitting in a corner on the one blanket they now shared and said nothing.

At lunch that day, the man ate only part of his soup, then lay down and fell asleep. Cornet glanced back and forth between the sleeping man and his soup and found himself tempted to consume the rest. He crouched next to the bowl and began to eat spoonful after spoonful until the man's soup was gone. A while later, the man woke up. He picked up his bowl, noticed that it was empty, and—completely oblivious to Cornet—went back to his corner to sit on the blanket.

Cornet wondered, "Does he know that I ate his soup and he doesn't dare say anything? . . . But there is one thing I know! The methods used by the Nazis had managed to make me forget my human dignity. Confinement, beatings, hunger had been pushed to such a level of sophistication that I lost what differentiated me from an animal."

At that moment, he decided to never again let the Nazis turn him into such a monster.

27

THE BUNKER

The hallway leading to the bunker.

The *Arrestanten* placed in solitary-confinement cells did not divulge as much information as the SS desired, so a more drastic measure was taken.

In August 1942, the camp administration, with the encouragement of the SIPO-SD, had decided to refurbish an isolated, odd-shaped room near the *Revier*. The room became known as the bunker; in reality, it was the torture chamber, where the *Arrestanten* could be coerced to give up the names and addresses of accomplices.

———

How a prisoner was taken to the bunker was a kind of torture in itself. An *Arrestant,* his head covered with the blue bag, might be taken from his cell in the morning at the time he regularly visited the toilet. On the way, he might be directed to turn left instead of right, then pushed down a small hallway where he was stopped and told to wait. As he stood in this unfamiliar

Once the prisoner's hood was removed, he would see torture instruments lying on a nearby table.

place, the torment began . . . as he heard another prisoner, around the corner, being tortured first. The screams echoed in the small area—indeed, the screams reverberated throughout the concrete hallways of the fort—so that the waiting *Arrestant* was already in agony simply by awaiting his turn.

In the bunker, the cloth bag was pulled off the prisoner's head, allowing him to perceive the shock of his new surroundings. First, he might see a bare room with a small stove and a table. On the table, he might notice a typewriter for recording a confession. Then his eyes might focus on the smaller details, such as the objects that might help reward or extract a confession: food, cigarettes, a gun, a truncheon, a whip, and other, more gruesome torture tools. Finally, he might observe an iron hook that hung from the ceiling, and a narrow, curved trench cut into the concrete floor for carrying bodily fluids toward a drain against the outer wall.

"You will talk," the prisoner might be told, "if not today, then tomorrow, and if not tomorrow, then the day after. But you will talk."

The first visit might be for intimidation. Sometimes the SS would let the prisoner imagine how bad the bunker might be and give him time to talk. Other times, the first visit to the bunker was the worst and the torture was such that the prisoner passed out, only to be brought to, still in the room, for another round.

No matter what the first session was like, the prisoner was often told that he could expect a return visit to the bunker. That way, he could never relax when he heard boots stomping or keys jangling in the hallway outside his cell.

———

One of the most detailed accounts of torture in Breendonk was written many years later by the Austrian-born prisoner Hans Mayer. His father was Jewish; his mother converted to Judaism when she married. In 1938, after the *Anschluss* and *Kristallnacht,* an old friend who had become a Nazi warned Mayer that he

Hans Mayer.

should disappear from Austria because of his Jewish heritage.

But disappearing was not easy, since Mayer could not leave without the proper papers, including a passport and a visa. He made contact with another friend, who volunteered to help provide him with documents under two conditions: Mayer must divorce his Jewish wife, and his mother must declare that Mayer's father was actually an Aryan man with whom she committed adultery.

Mayer refused.

He and his wife finally escaped in late 1938 by traveling legally to Cologne, Germany, where they paid a man to smuggle them across the Belgian border. In Belgium, Mayer and his wife made a new life for themselves. After the German invasion, he worked as a moving man and sometimes as a German teacher at a Jewish school. In his spare time, he wrote articles and edited the newspaper for a communist resistance group. He also helped distribute the paper, primarily in places where German troops might find it. Mayer and his friends hoped that the *Wehrmacht* soldiers who read it would become aware of the true nature of Hitler's war.

On July 23, 1943, shortly after placing mimeographed newspapers with the headline "DEATH TO THE SS BANDITS AND GESTAPO HANGMEN!" in front of a German army barrack, Mayer was arrested by the SIPO-SD. He had always imagined that SIPO-SD agents would have "twisted noses, hypertrophied chins, pockmarks, and knife scars." He was surprised that they had looked quite ordinary.

Taken first to SIPO-SD headquarters, he was questioned about the names and addresses of the other people in his resistance group.

"If you talk," he was told, "then you will be put in a military police prison. If you don't confess, then it's off to Breendonk, and you know what that means."

He divulged nothing. In fact, he had nothing to tell them, even if he wanted to confess, because he knew only the code names of his compatriots. As a punishment for his refusal to talk, he was struck for the first time. Twenty years later, he described that moment in an essay. He was shocked by the assault, by the complete disregard for human dignity, and yet he was surprised that the blow did not hurt more. The agents hit him again and again, but each blow to his body was "its own anesthetic. A feeling of pain that would be comparable to a violent toothache or the pulsating burning of a festering wound does not emerge. For that reason, the beaten person thinks roughly this: Well, now, this can be put up with; hit me as much as you want, it will get you nowhere."

He did not confess, and he was taken to Breendonk later that day.

———

Mayer knew about prewar German concentration camps, where political opponents of the Nazis as well as habitual criminals were incarcerated. As a writer with a vivid imagination, he was able to picture in his mind what lay ahead for him at Breendonk: "prison, interrogation, blows, torture; in the end, most probably death."

What waited for him initially was SS-Lieutenant Prauss, who greeted him in the registration office with a three-foot-long leather horsewhip dangling from his wrist.

"Now it's coming," he told Mayer.

The hook was attached to the handcuffs that held a prisoner's arms behind his back. Then the hook was raised so that the prisoner dangled above the floor.

Prauss and two SIPO-SD agents then led him down the corridor, past the barracks, past the *Revier,* until they reached the bunker.

There, Mayer was placed beneath the iron hook hanging from the vaulted ceiling on a rope that looped through a pulley. The hook was lowered and attached to the iron shackles that bound his hands behind his back. Next, the hook was raised, lifting Mayer some three feet off the floor. For a few minutes, he struggled to hold his arms down behind his back. At the same time, his tormentors asked him questions about his accomplices and their addresses. He could not answer as he concentrated on his immediate survival.

Soon, his muscles failed, as they would for anyone, and his arms were yanked up, behind his back, over his head. He felt "a crackling and splintering in my shoulders that my body has not forgotten until this hour. The balls sprang from their sockets . . . I fell into a void and now hung by my dislocated arms, which had been torn high from behind and were now twisted over my head. What visual instruction in etymology! At the same time, the blows from the horsewhip showered down on my body, and some of them sliced cleanly through the light summer trousers that I was wearing."

The torturers paused and smoked a cigarette as Mayer

These blocks were placed beneath the hook. At times, the SS would release the dangling prisoner without warning and drop him onto the blocks, severely bruising or even breaking his legs.

dangled over the floor, still conscious. He realized that if he had known the real names of his compatriots, he would have revealed them. And he did talk, inventing bizarre crimes that he pretended to have committed.

Finally, he passed out.

The bunker at Breendonk.

When he woke up, the torture had stopped. He was taken to his new home, Cell 13, where he remained for many months, until he was transported out of Belgium to another concentration camp.

————

Mayer's experience in the bunker was not unusual or unique, but torture did not necessarily produce the results the SS wanted. "It's easy to make a person scream," one prisoner said. "But few of us talked." Still, the SS kept trying, and many prisoners were brutalized there, including many of the thirty or so women who were imprisoned at the camp. One was Marguerite Paquet, taken to Breendonk on January 9, 1943, accused of being a spy.

Marguerite Paquet shows the scars from cigarette burns that the SS gave her in the bunker.

In handcuffs twenty-four hours a day, Paquet was placed in Cell 16 of Barrack 8, where she was made to stand from six a.m. until eight p.m. daily. She was interrogated, stripped naked, and tortured in the bunker some seven times by SS-Major Schmitt, SS-Lieutenant Prauss, and SS Wyss and De Bodt. When she was transferred to another prison in October 1943, she was placed in a cell with another prisoner, who saw firsthand the results of the torture at Breendonk: the tips of Paquet's fingers had been crushed so badly that her nails had fallen out. Her arms, legs, and back were covered with bruises and cigarette burns.

After the war, Paquet described her torture to a commission studying the atrocities at Breendonk. Near the end of the first interrogation, she explained that she was given an injection "intended to stupefy" her. She explained, "I took advantage of a moment's inattention to put my fingers down my throat thus making myself vomit."

She heard the man who had administered the injection tell Major Schmitt, "It's no good, the injection makes her sick." Still, she was tortured on six more occasions. Every day, she received "punches and truncheon blows which, among other things, broke my teeth. In the course of the daily outing to empty the bucket I received a bayonet wound in the arm, the sentry thinking that I was lifting up my hood." Another time, when she tried to look out from under the blue bag over her head, she was hit in the neck with a rifle butt, which broke three vertebrae.

This torture instrument was used to crush Marguerite Paquet's fingers.

Eventually, she was sent to Ravensbrück, a concentration camp for women in Germany.

———

Even those lucky enough to survive the torture were never the same. Years later, Hans Mayer wrote, "[Every day] I am still dangling over the ground by dislocated arms, panting, and accusing myself."

28

JANUARY 6, 1943

From November 1942 through March 1943, sixty-eight prisoners were executed at Breendonk.

On the morning of January 5, SS De Bodt entered the prisoner Victor Trido's barrack and selected twenty men to follow him. When the men returned a few hours later, they explained that De Bodt had ordered them to prepare the execution site by scraping away the snow, building up the sand behind the execution posts, and removing any blood from the previous executions. De Bodt also warned the men that any of them might well be tied to one of the posts and shot one day.

Because Trido had just arrived at the camp, he worried that he might be slated for execution, but he was not alone in this fear. Practically every inmate at Breendonk harbored the same thought, and their conversations that day and their dreams that night were tortured by the possibility of another execution. They did not know that the *Militärverwaltung* had already decided to execute twenty hostages the next day. Ten would be shot in retaliation for bomb attacks against the Germans that had taken place in Brussels during December. The second ten would be executed in reprisal for the murder of collaborators that had occurred on the night of January 1.

On January 6, SS-Lieutenant Prauss and De Bodt entered Trido's barrack and ordered the prisoners to attention. As they lined up at the foot of their beds, expecting the worst, all they received were random lashes of the whip.

"You'll get to know Breendonk!" De Bodt told them before they left.

A short time later, they heard SS officers and guards pushing a group of ten prisoners down the hall to Room 1. Then, from their windows, they saw two trucks from the Belgian Red Cross drive into the courtyard, carrying a cargo of coffins. Not long after, *Wehrmacht* soldiers escorted the now-shirtless prisoners from Room 1 to the execution ground. Their hands were tied, and their coats were placed over their shoulders. Soon the men in Trido's room heard a volley of rifle shots, followed by silence, then individual gunshots as any of the men who were still alive were given another bullet to the head, a coup de grâce.

When the soldiers returned to Room 1, they took the second group of condemned men to their deaths on the execution ground.

But the day was not over.

―――――

At eleven o'clock that evening, Trido and the other men in his barrack were suddenly awakened by the sounds of a prisoner being beaten. They heard "the noise of a whip falling forcefully . . . [and] the screams of death." Although they did not know it, a prisoner named Jacob Hilbolling, a member of a Soviet spy ring called the Red Orchestra, was murdered that night by the SS and was most likely the man whose cries they heard.

Finally, all was quiet. As the men tried to go back to sleep, they heard footsteps in the hallway and their barrack door being unlocked. The door flew open, and in strutted an SS officer and De Bodt, both drunk and looking for trouble. They called the men to attention without giving them time to pull on their pants. Then they began to strike the prisoners.

"So ended the day of January 6, 1943," Trido wrote, "marked by twenty executions, a murder committed in a solitary confinement cell . . . and scenes of unspeakable brutality committed by a senior officer in the German army and a Belgian traitor to his country, the SS De Bodt."

―――――

A similar episode occurred a week later, on January 13.

Shortly before six a.m., Trido and the other prisoners in his barrack saw ten prisoners pass through the courtyard, stripped to the waist, beaten as they were marched to the execution ground. One man was carried there on a stretcher. Trido learned that the day before, as the man was being transferred from a Brussels prison to Breendonk, he tried to escape by jumping out of the truck and broke his foot.

The other condemned men walked with their heads held high. "In their minds," Trido imagined, "they saw the school where as a child they learned to love their country. They saw the image of an affectionate mother, an adored father, a sister, a brother that they loved, a beloved wife, precious children." By focusing on the memories of their loved ones, they could avoid seeing the soldiers, the execution posts, and the coffins that were stacked nearby. Even the man with the broken foot managed to stand upright when he was tied to his post, smiling at the soldiers, despite the pain he was surely in.

After their execution, another ten were marched to the execution ground and shot as well.

———

Paul Colin.

In less than four months, from late November to mid-March, sixty-eight prisoners were executed at Breendonk, but these were just the beginning. The next execution, held on May 10, shocked many Belgians. This time, a trio of condemned men would be hanged.

The men—André Bertulot, Maurice Raskin, and Arnaud Fraiteur—had murdered Paul Colin, a well-known Belgian journalist and newspaper editor whose writings vehemently touted the new order that the Nazis desired. One Belgian described him as "the cleverest, meanest, most unscrupulous, and most influential" collaborating journalist in Belgium. Some members of the resistance seemed to follow

Arnaud Fraiteur, Maurice Raskin, and André Bertulot were sentenced to death and hanged at Breendonk.

the motto "Resist the Nazi torturers and strike their accomplices." Colin became their target on April 14.

During the attack, Fraiteur fired the gun, but the trio's escape was thwarted. Bertulot was apprehended almost immediately; Raskin the next day. Neither informed the SIPO-SD about Fraiteur, but an abandoned bicycle, registered in his name and discovered near Colin's office, had been found soon after the shooting. Two weeks later, occupation authorities caught Fraiteur.

The three were badly tortured. They received a quick trial, but the outcome was already predetermined. The men would be found guilty and hanged, the first time such a method of execution had been used in Belgium in more than 150 years. Because most Belgians considered hanging to be barbaric, the *Militärverwaltung* hoped that such a drastic response would deter the intensifying wave of deadly attacks by the resistance.

The gallows at Breendonk.

Anyone, they said, who committed an act of violence against German soldiers or their sympathizers would be hanged from then on.

On May 10, the men were executed at Breendonk on a three-position gallows directly across from the wooden posts of the firing squad. Two days later, it was announced in the Belgian press that the men had been hanged for "the dastardly, cowardly nature" of their crime. Despite the military administration's wishes, the assassination of Colin produced the opposite result: many collaborating journalists, now afraid for their lives, "abandoned their violently aggressive character."

29

THE WINTER OF
1942–43

The moat in winter.

The bleakest and deadliest winter at Breendonk occurred from December 1942 to March 1943. As it became clearer that Germany might lose World War II, the SS officers and guards at the camp became even angrier in their dealings with the prisoners. Led by one of their senior officers, they began to vent their frustrations on the prisoners in unbelievably cruel ways.

SS-First Lieutenant Johann Kantschuster

That senior officer, SS-First Lieutenant Johann Kantschuster, had filled in as acting commandant from September 1942 to April 1943 while SS-Major Schmitt tended to the *Sammellager* in Mechelen. Many prisoners who survived both Prauss and Kantschuster declared that the latter was much worse.

Kantschuster established his reputation on his third day at the camp, when he began to beat the prisoner Oscar Beck on the work site. Beck raised his hands to protect his face and pleaded with him to stop. Instead, Kantschuster pulled out his revolver and, without any hesitation, shot him dead. During a quick inquiry afterward, Kantschuster claimed that Beck had threatened him. Prisoners who witnessed the shooting, though, knew that no such thing had happened.

Oscar Beck.

The prisoners quickly learned that Kantschuster was inebriated by eight o'clock most mornings and that his drunkenness only added to his cruelty. One day in the camp kitchen, he knocked a prisoner to the floor, then poured a can of boiling "acorn coffee" on him, scalding him severely.

But it was during the winter of 1942–43, when Germany was in the throes of losing the prolonged and bloody Battle of Stalingrad, that Kantschuster earned his reputation as a "real beast." According to Dr. Singer, he blamed the Jews for the German defeat at Stalingrad, and so he instigated a series of murders as an act of revenge. At least fourteen prisoners—all but one a Jew—were murdered by the side of the moat from late January through early March 1943, including four who were killed in one day. The victims were reportedly all selected by Kantschuster, who ordered his henchmen, SS Wyss and De Bodt, to carry out the brutal murders.

On January 27, for example, Wyss and De Bodt called three prisoners to them at the worksite, then beat them with their fists and whips. When the prisoners fell to the ground, they were kicked until they were bloody and could not move. When the lunch whistle sounded, they were carried back to their barrack, but they were not allowed to remain there. After lunch, prisoners were ordered to carry them back to the work site. The men's faces were swollen, their arms hung limply at their sides, blood oozed from their mouths. The prisoners were told to place them on the banks of the moat.

Then Wyss and De Bodt shoved the men into the icy water, pulled them out, and buried them up to their necks in the sand. "Nothing could be worse," wrote Victor Trido, a witness to the torture, "than watching these three heads sticking out of the ground, and yet the SS laughed!"

The three men had tears in their eyes, but that did not stop Wyss and De Bodt from shoveling sand onto their faces, as if they were competing to see who could bury the men first. But Wyss and De Bodt were not finished. They dug the men up, stripped off their clothing, and coated the men's bodies with mud until they were unrecognizable. Again the two SS

Nusem Zybenberg.

could not stop. They stuffed the men's mouths, their ears, and their eyes with mud. Finally, they grabbed shovels and beat the men until they were dead.

Although Trido described the murders of three men that day, only two deaths were written into the record: Philippe Lamm and Nusem Zybenberg. Whether the name of the third man was lost or destroyed over time or Victor Trido was mistaken about the number is unknown. But the official cause of death was clearly reported: "depression and weak circulation."

On March 5, a similar scene occurred beside the moat. Hugo Schönagel was murdered along with Wolf Hartlooper, Albert Spiero, and Jacques Loitzanski. Loitzanski's sister, Aline, had already been a prisoner at Breendonk, on her way to the *Sammellager* in Mechelen and then to Auschwitz-Birkenau. A fifth man, never identified, survived.

Hugo Schönagel.

Not all of these men left behind documents that revealed what their lives were like before they were incarcerated at Breendonk, but Schönagel's immigration records provided a glimpse. Born in Vienna, he worked as a chauffeur. After the *Anschluss* in March 1938, Schönagel, like many Austrian Jews, was singled out for abuse. In May 1938, he arrived in Belgium and applied for political-refugee status. To obtain this, Schönagel had to explain the reason for his request. He wrote about his experience in Vienna in a matter-of-fact way: "I had a discussion with a Nazi. I was beaten and forced to clear the streets. I underwent other punishments, and afraid of being arrested, I fled." Schönagel believed that he had found a safer place in Belgium, away from the terror of the Nazis.

The SS at Breendonk proved that wrong.

———————

The only known non-Jew killed by the moat that winter was seventeen-year-old Auguste Leleu.

On the freezing morning of March 9, 1943, the prisoners were on the work site. They had been commanded to remove their jackets, as was often done in the winter, simply to make them suffer more.

Wyss and De Bodt spied young Auguste Leleu.

"You can't work any faster?" De Bodt asked him.

"I'm cold, Mr. SS Man," the teenager replied.

De Bodt burst out laughing and said to Wyss, "Wyss, Leleu is cold."

Wyss said, "Throw him in the water. That will warm him up."

De Bodt shoved Leleu in the moat. When he tried to climb out, De Bodt pushed him back in. Once again, Leleu approached the edge of the moat, this time begging them to stop their torture. He was freezing. Instead, the two Flemish SS beat him and buried him up to his neck in sand, as they had done to so many others. They ordered the other prisoners on the work site to parade past him while Leleu cried for his mother.

Around lunch, they allowed some prisoners to dig him up and carry him to the barrack, but soon Wyss and De Bodt took him from his room to the showers, where they placed him naked under a stream of icy water.

Auguste Leleu.

When they were done, he was taken back to his room.

Auguste Leleu died a few hours later.

––––––––––

On April 8, after the terrible winter was finally over, SS-Major Schmitt was dismissed as the commandant of SS-*Sammellager* Mechelen. Tailoring—and greed—were his downfall.

Schmitt had purchased large quantities of fabric and leather and then put Jewish tailors incarcerated at the *Sammellager* to work, sometimes thirteen hours a day, making clothing and leather accessories, such as belts and purses. Schmitt sold the items and pocketed the money. When he was turned in by a fellow SS officer, he claimed that he had shared the profits with the SIPO-SD, although there was no proof of this.

Despite this setback, he was still permitted to keep his post at Breendonk, at least for a while.

As for SS-Lieutenant Kantschuster, he was removed from Breendonk for unknown reasons that same April.

30

TRANSPORT XX

A photograph of the exterior of the former SS-Sammellager-Mechelen (now the Kazerne Dossin Museum) taken about 1950 still showed the train tracks in the foreground where prisoners were loaded on the transports for Auschwitz-Birkenau.

After Schmitt's removal as commandant of the *Sammellager,* the next planned deportation train to Auschwitz-Birkenau was Transport XX, scheduled to leave Mechelen on the evening of April 19, 1943, with 1,631 men, women, and children. At least sixteen Breendonk prisoners were aboard, including early Room 1 prisoners Israel Steinberg, Ernest Landau, and prisoner number 59, Hermann Kahn. Transport XX also included the father, mother, and ninety-year-old great-uncle of Charlotte Hamburger.

Transport XX was different from the others. The first nineteen trains had used cars with third-class compartments, which allowed some people to escape by jumping out the doors of the poorly guarded trains. This time, the SS had decided to use freight cars with sliding doors. Once the prisoners were inside, the door would be closed and secured with wire. Because these cars were not even intended for animals, there was no adequate ventilation, simply two metal grates placed high on the wall, covered by hatches. The SS believed it would be practically impossible to break out of these cars, so only one officer and fifteen German police, stationed in the front and rear cars, were assigned to guard the train.

The change to freight cars did not deter many of the passengers, who stockpiled tools that might help them escape from the train. One prisoner, Régine Krochmal, was even told just before the train departed that it was headed for Auschwitz and secretly handed a knife to help her escape.

But Transport XX would be different for another reason: an outside resistance group planned to attack this transport and free as many prisoners as possible.

———

The daring idea to attack the train was conceived by Hertz Jospa, a leader of the communist resistance in Belgium, and

carried out by three young men: former high school friends

Youra Livchitz, Jean Franklemon, and Robert
Maistriau. Youra's older brother, Alexandre,
had also wanted to help, but he was out of
commission; he had been wounded attempting to assassinate the head of the Belgian
Central Police, a known collaborator. Now
Alexandre was recuperating in a hospital
under an assumed name for protection, so the
three friends decided to act alone.

Youra Livchitz

In their simple plan, they would stop
the train by tricking the engineer with a red
emergency lantern. As it rounded a bend
near Boortmeerbeek, a village about seven
miles from Mechelen, the engineer would
spy the light they had placed on the tracks
and be forced to apply the brakes. Then the
three young men would help the passengers
escape.

Jean Franklemon.

Early in the evening of April 19, they rode
their bicycles from Brussels to the designated
spot. Livchitz and Franklemon walked up the
tracks in the direction of the approaching train.
Maistriau headed away from them, carrying an
oil lantern with its glass covered in red tissue
paper, and placed it on the tracks. Franklemon
and Maistriau both had pliers to cut open the
locked carriages; Livchitz brought a gun, which
he would fire to make the Germans believe
that they were under attack. Once they were in
position, they moved into the woods that lined
the tracks and waited.

Robert Maistriau.

Before the train departed from Mechelen
at ten p.m., the prisoners on Transport XX had

been warned by the SS that if anyone escaped, everyone else would be "shot on arrival." A Jewish monitor, a *chef de wagon,* was even assigned to each car to make certain that everyone obeyed the directive. But that did not stop the prisoners who had smuggled tools aboard. Just after the train left Mechelen, two boys used a hacksaw to remove one of the hatches in their car and quickly jumped. Régine Krochmal, in a medical car near the back, stood on a suitcase and, using the knife she had been given, opened the hatch and jumped. Many other prisoners were waiting to escape when the train reached the country-side, unaware that it was about to be stopped.

As the train approached the bend near Boortmeerbeek, the engineer saw a glowing red light ahead. Believing that it signaled an emergency, the engineer applied the brakes, and the train squealed loudly to a stop. Maistriau ran to the first car in front of him and opened the door with his pliers. He shone a flashlight on the people inside.

"Get out, get out!" he yelled first in French, then in German.

Two women jumped, including Hena Wasyng, a house-wife from Antwerp whose husband had been killed by the SIPO-SD and whose two young sons were in hiding. She recalled, "[A] man from the Resistance opened the door of our wagon. . . . I was frightened, afraid to jump, but I changed my mind: if I didn't jump, then my children would be left all alone."

Another woman, perhaps the *chef de wagon,* tried to block the door, ordering the others to stay. But not all obeyed. Maistriau moved on to the next car, but the moonlight was bright that night, and the Germans began to fire at him. As the train began to move on, he ran into the woods where some of the people had gathered, and handed them some money to use in their escape.

At the center of the train, Franklemon had not fared well. He had just begun to cut the wire closure on one of the cars when he heard a German policeman say, *Hände hoch!* "Put your hands up!"

When he turned to look, he saw a uniformed man, some one hundred feet away, pointing a rifle at him. Franklemon took a chance and began to run. The policeman caught up to him and tried to hit him with his rifle, but Franklemon punched him first, and the officer fell.

Eventually, Franklemon and Maistriau met at the place where they had hidden their bicycles, but Livchitz was nowhere to be found. Later, they learned that, after he had fired his gun a few times when the train stopped, two German policemen had chased him. Afraid to return to the bicycles, he had chosen to walk back to Brussels.

———

In the end, they weren't able to free as many people as they had hoped. Only seventeen had escaped from the first car that Maistriau had opened before the train continued on its way. By the time it reached the German border, however, 231 others had fled the train. Of those, however, twenty-six were killed in the attempt, and another ninety recaptured.

One of the escapees was none other than Israel Steinberg, the keeper of the pigsty at Breendonk. By the next morning, he had found his way back to Brussels, where he went into hiding and tried to make ends meet as best he could. At about ten in the morning on June 24, 1943, he was caught stealing a wallet containing 132 Belgian francs from a woman on the tram. Taken into custody, he was also found to have a false identity card, for a man named Alberto Ferrari. He was put in a Belgian jail, under Belgian authority—away from the SS— where he remained throughout the rest of the war.

Ernest Landau and Hermann Kahn did not escape from

Transport XX, perhaps because the prisoners in their car could not open the hatch. When they arrived at Auschwitz-Birkenau, the SS opened the door of their car and shouted, *Raus, raus aus den Wagons.* "Get out, get out of the wagon."

The prisoners began to jump from the train car, but a woman, holding her baby, needed help. An SS guard snatched the infant from her arms and flung it against a rock, killing it. When the woman threw herself at the man, she was shot.

Then the selection process began. As Landau and Kahn, side by side, reached the front of the inspection line, the officer hesitated when he looked at the fifty-year-old Kahn.

"Can you walk?"

"Well, with difficulty," Kahn replied honestly.

As Landau listened, he realized that it was a trick question. Perhaps he remembered what an SS lieutenant had told him before the departure of Transport XX: "So far you've had it

A memorial near the Boortmeerbeek railway station today honors the memory of the prisoners on Transport XX.

easy but where you're headed now, you're in for a very nasty surprise. That is, if any of you have time."

When Landau was asked the same question, he told the SS officer, "Yes, sir."

"And can you run?"

"Of course."

Then the SS officer reached a decision: Kahn was directed to a waiting bus, while Landau was sent to the camp on foot. There, he was registered, and his left forearm was tattooed with his prisoner number, 117601. He later learned that the buses had gone directly to the gas chamber.

31.

THE CHAPLAIN OF THE EXECUTIONS

Today some visitors to Breendonk leave flowers by the execution posts in memory of those who died there.

On July 13, three new prisoners—badly beaten—arrived at Breendonk, sent from a prison in Liège, Belgium. They spoke only French and did not understand any of the German commands that the SS barked at them. All were communists and members of the resistance. The prisoner Pierre Stippelmans, a Catholic, had "never heard great things about the communists." But when one of the men, whose bunk was above his, asked him to join in prayer, he agreed.

The man sat on Stippelmans's bunk all night, gripping his hand, trying to tell his story. Stipplemans, a Dutch speaker, could not understand most of what the man was saying, but he could tell that he was in great distress.

————

Early on the morning of July 14, the prisoners of another barrack realized that something was unusual: the breakfast coffee was late. Victor Trido and his friend Paul discussed the possible reason: it was Bastille Day in France. Although it was not celebrated in Belgium, they joked that perhaps the camp administration had decided to give them a holiday.

Trido didn't mind the delay, though, because the longer it took for their coffee to arrive, the less time they would have to work outside. But Paul wanted his coffee, because he had developed a special routine. Every night, when he received his evening ration of bread, he would cut it into very thin slices. Then he would eat only a few and save the rest for the morning.

Suddenly, there was noise from the hallway—a good sign, they thought. When an SS officer and two guards entered, the prisoners jumped to attention. Then the officer unexpectedly announced Paul's number.

Paul seemed pleased. "They came to find me so I could be released," he said confidently, and handed Trido his extra slices of bread.

Trido placed the bread on the table and turned briefly to watch his friend's departure. Paul waved goodbye and left with the guards. When Trido looked back at the table, someone had stolen the bread.

The coffee still did not arrive; the fort seemed unusually silent.

———

In Pierre Stippelmans's barrack, an SS officer arrived and, in German, announced the numbers of the French-speaking men who had arrived the day before. Because the men from Liège did not understand what he was saying, the officer explained that they had been sentenced to death. As soon as the officer finished, *Zugführer* Obler tied the men's hands behind their backs. Then they were marched away.

———

In all, nine numbers were called that morning. The condemned prisoners were taken to the SS canteen, a large room off the main entrance tunnel where the SS ate their meals and sometimes held parties.

Monsignor Otto Gramann.

In the canteen that day was Monsignor Otto Gramann, the chaplain general of the *Wehrmacht* in Belgium. It was his responsibility to meet with prisoners who were condemned to death. At other Belgian prisons, he was able to spend the final night before the execution speaking to the prisoner. At Breendonk, however, he was allowed only the final hour with the condemned men.

During his allotted hour, Gramann heard a last confession if the prisoner was Catholic, though he offered solace and comfort to all. He also brought paper with him so that each prisoner could write a final letter to his family. Any letters written by condemned prisoners at Breendonk, however, had to be given to SS-Major Schmitt; most were not sent, Gramann testified later, perhaps because "all of them ended with the words 'Long Live Belgium.'" Many prisoners were touched by the kindness and sensitivity shown by Gramann.

Remarkably, he kept a diary that documented the details of many of the executions. In his July 14 entry, he described the last hour of the prisoners by first expressing his surprise at being asked to hear the confession of a Protestant. The man, he wrote, "makes a very long prayer of repentance, kneeling, his face in his hands."

He explained that the men, seated at a table in the canteen, wrote final letters. Next, "cheese, sandwiches, and coffee are brought to the table. I give them cigarettes. They have to be done in one hour." Finally, an SS lieutenant—perhaps Prauss—entered and read their official sentence.

When one of the men collapsed on the floor, the lieutenant kicked him. Afterward, the men were marched silently to the execution site: "They have to take off all their clothes, except for their shoes and socks. . . . They are quickly tied to the stake." Although the men at every execution asked not to be blindfolded, the officer in charge always refused for fear that if "the condemned men looked the soldiers in the eyes, they would become nervous and no longer know how to shoot."

That day, two of the men begin to sing "The Internationale," a communist anthem meant to defy the Germans. Another man, a Belgian police officer named Georges Van Wassenhove who had aided the resistance, shouted, "Long live the king!"

Georges Van Wassenhove.

"Long live Belgium!" the other eight men yelled in response.

The *Wehrmacht* officer in charge was so unnerved by their defiance that he ordered the soldiers to fire before they were ready. As a result, many of the shots missed their target. "All of them," Gramann wrote, "need another shot to finish them off, some even two or three. . . . They get thrown into coffins—their shoes get yanked off. . . . Before and after there is cognac for the officers. Schmitt didn't show up."

Before the *Wehrmacht* soldiers could leave the execution ground, their guns had to be inspected to make certain that they had performed their duty by firing their rifles.

———

In the barracks, the prisoners had heard the burst of shots, followed by single gunshots to the men who were still breathing. Moments later, Obler arrived in Pierre Stippelmans's room, carrying the bloody ropes that had tied the men to the execution posts.

Sadly, Stippelmans realized that he "did not even know the name of the man who had talked to me for hours. . . . God rest your soul, dear friend."

———

Many years later, in 1971 and 1972, former members of the *Wehrmacht* who had participated in the firing squad executions at Breendonk were questioned in a German court.

Sixty-eight-year-old Johann G. told the court that he and the other soldiers "were just implementers."

"We had no influence on the event," he continued. "I was too scared for that. I did also not want to be killed myself for refusing to obey. I was then already married and a father. A poor man like me had nothing to say about the orders we were given."

He had been one of the shooters in the July 14, 1943, execution and remembered that some of the condemned men had sung "The Internationale." According to the lawyer who questioned him, during his appearance in court Johann G. "was at times in tears and repeated each time how terrible it was to shoot defenseless people."

Another soldier who participated in the same execution, Johann K., remembered how the hostages were singing loudly when the officer in charge yelled, "Ready, set, fire." As a result, the soldiers did not hear the command well enough, "and the shootings lacked precision. This is how one of the men was hit only in the arm. He then shouted: 'Dirty German pigs, shoot me again!' I've always been amazed at their courage and defiance in the face of death. . . . You would have thought that they were happy to be executed."

32

TWO HEROES
OF BREENDONK

Saint-Gilles Prison in Brussels.

As the momentum of the war turned against Germany, life at Breendonk continued to change. By September 1943, most Jews had been sent to the *Sammellager* in Mechelen and transported to Auschwitz-Birkenau; only a few remained at Breendonk. Even *Zugführer* Obler was deported. SS-Major Schmitt reportedly told him, "Now you know too much, so we are going to liquidate you." That began his journey through a number of prisons and concentration camps, including Auschwitz, Sachsenhausen, and finally Mauthausen.

SS-Major Karl Schönwetter.

That fall, about four hundred prisoners were incarcerated at Breendonk. Perhaps demoralized by his downfall at the *Sammellager,* Schmitt began taking sick leave. At the end of November, he was finally replaced as commandant by SS-Major Karl Schönwetter.

———

Among the prisoners that fall was Youra Livchitz.

A month after the April attack on Transport XX, Livchitz, still active in the resistance, was set up by a double agent and arrested by the SIPO-SD. At its headquarters, he was handcuffed and beaten with a pistol during his interrogation. That night, left alone in a cell, he managed to remove a safety pin on the underside of his jacket lapel and picked the lock on one side of his handcuffs. Then he lay down on the floor, clutched his stomach, and began to moan loudly. After the guard had entered his cell, Livchitz knocked him out and took his gun and uniform. He fled to the house of his girlfriend and her parents, but Youra was a wanted man. So was his brother, Alexandre, since he had been identified as the would-be assassin of the police superintendent.

The two brothers made arrangements to be smuggled

out of Belgium in a delivery truck headed for northern France. From there, they would be taken to England. But on June 26, the day they were to begin their journey, the German military police stopped delivery trucks leaving Brussels and found the two brothers. They were taken to Breendonk, where both were probably tortured and kept in solitary confinement.

At seven thirty in the morning of January 12, 1944, Alexandre was taken from his room and sent to the Saint-Gilles Prison in Brussels; he was not allowed to say goodbye to his brother. There he was tried, convicted, and sentenced to death for the attempted assassination of the police superintendent.

As he awaited his execution, Monsignor Gramann visited him. On the night of February 8, he dined on his last meal of "coffee, a jar of fish paste, and biscuits" and had the opportunity to write a letter. In part, he wrote:

> For two hours now I have known for certain that I will be executed tomorrow morning at eight o'clock. One more rotation of the hands, and at last I will be free. I am calm, and when I was read the confirmation of the sentence as well as the rejection of my request for mercy, I didn't bat an eyelid. . . . I may say . . . that I will go to the firing post (for I am being shot—at least it's better than being hanged) with my head held high, without regrets, . . . with a sense of having tried to do my best to fight for a better life and for the beginning of a new world. I shall not end this letter without saying to you—and that as someone who is not at all a believer—that emotionally I do not believe in the absolute nothing; I have no particular love of anything hypothetical, but it is hard for me to admit that I will fall into the black hole that has appeared to me in my feverish dreams. . . . That is all to tell you that my life will go on existing apart from my earthly body, perhaps in someone else or somewhere else. Who knows?

The next morning, he was executed, not at Breendonk but at a site in Brussels called the Tir National, a military shooting

The Tir National, a military shooting range, was the site of many executions by the Militärverwaltung *during World War II.*

range that was used as execution grounds by the German occupier.

During the week that followed, his brother, Youra, was selected to die in reprisal for bombing attacks on German offices. Monsignor Gramann also visited him and offered him the chance to write a final letter.

Youra addressed it to his mother:

> Even if words are powerless to express all that I feel, I am leaving this cell to go toward the other side with a calmness . . . that is also a resignation in facing the inevitable. To tell you that I regret everything that has happened would serve nothing. I regret much more that I am no longer there to help you. . . . I would like so much to be there so that together we could work toward a better future.

Dear Mama, do not cry too much when you think of me. My life till now has been very full. . . . Remember me without pain. . . . I must say goodbye to you, time is passing so quickly. Once again, it is not the last moments that were the hardest. Be confident and courageous in life, time erases many things. . . .

Your son who loves you, Youra

A week after his brother's death, Youra was also executed by firing squad at the Tir National.

———

A few days later, Youra's girlfriend received a strange request from the *Militärverwaltung*. She was to go to the headquarters at the Place Royale in Brussels. There, at the appointed time, Monsignor Gramann was waiting for her with the letters that the two brothers had written.

"They both died as heroes," he told her.

As military chaplain, he had witnessed both executions. He told her that Youra had rejected the possibility of having a blindfold.

He preferred to watch the sunrise at the moment of his death.

———

As for Jean Franklemon and Robert Maistriau, who helped stop Transport XX, they too were arrested and sent to Breendonk. After a time, they were transferred to concentration camps in Germany.

THE TWELVE
FROM SENZEILLES

Photographs of the twelve prisoners from Senzeilles are displayed today in the former SS canteen at Breendonk, the room in which they were sentenced to death.

Just days after Youra Livchitz was executed, a trial took place at Breendonk for twelve men from Senzeilles, a village in southern Belgium, who had been charged with the murder of three German soldiers.

One of the men was Albert Tielemans.

––––––––––

Albert Tielemans.

Life for Tielemans, like many Belgians, was difficult and confusing during the German occupation. Food was severely rationed, and many goods were in short supply. As a result, most Belgians suffered. A few, in their attempt to survive, saw an opportunity and chose either to steal or to collaborate with the Germans.

At first, Albert Tielemans was one of the opportunists. He committed a number of robberies around Antwerp, including the theft of ration books, which contained coupons that Belgians needed to trade for food. He claimed the robberies were done in the name of the resistance movement, but this was not the case; Tielemans benefited from the thefts. When the police prepared to arrest him, he fled in October 1943 to Senzeilles.

There, he changed his ways and actually began to work for the resistance, with an organization named Group G. He joined some of the members who lived in and operated out of the forest outside Senzeilles, where they had a fortified camp with huts, a kitchen, running water, and sentry posts. They stockpiled "arms and ammunition, terrorized traitors, [and] attacked trains and food convoys."

But their activities would come to an end soon after a B-17 bomber from the United States Air Force crashed in the forest on December 30, 1943. Group G helped the American fliers escape, but the Germans were interested in the wreckage and stationed three German soldiers to guard it. On February 8, 1944, they disappeared from their post. Not many days later, Group G sabotaged a nearby railway. Because these two events took place in the same vicinity, the German military became convinced that a resistance group was operating out of the forest.

On February 16, the military surrounded the forest with some five hundred soldiers carrying automatic weapons. Outmanned and outgunned, Albert Tielemans and the other partisans of Group G surrendered and, on February 25, were trucked to Breendonk, where the canteen was turned into a courtroom. At two p.m., the twelve were sentenced to death. Because three German soldiers had been killed, the *Militärverwaltung* chose the most brutal means of execution, only the second time that anyone had been hanged at the camp. At four p.m., the sentence was approved in Brussels. Shortly before six p.m., the men were taken to the execution ground.

———

After the war, Monsignor Gramann testified at a trial about the execution that day. The twelve men were divided into two equal groups. When the first six were taken to the gallows, only three could be hanged at a time. The others stood below, forced to watch. The first three hung from the rope for ten minutes before their bodies were removed and placed in nearby coffins. As the next three climbed up to the gallows, the men who had been executed first began to cry out in agony from their coffins; they were not dead.

"These hangings," Monsignor Gramann recalled, "were done by means of a rope which was fastened to a chain. The knots were very thick. It was explained to me that this was the cause of the long agony."

They were each given a final pistol shot.

The rest of the men were hanged for twenty minutes to make sure that they were dead. Afterward, the bodies were taken to Brussels and buried at a cemetery on the grounds of the Tir National.

The next day, the execution was announced in newspapers with the headline "DEATH SENTENCE AND EXECUTION OF 12 TERRORISTS." According to the article, an "autopsy revealed that the three soldiers were killed in a bestial way with blunt objects, and their bodies were buried in the forest after

Albert's brother (center) and mother (right) visited his grave in 1945.

Albert Tielemans's grave at the Tir National.

they had been stripped of their valuables." The point of the announcement, however, was its conclusion: "Terrorists should realize that the German army reacts quickly and with energy against all hostile and criminal elements. . . . This case should show once again to the Belgian population how it is wrong and dangerous to surround the terrorists with the vainglory of patriotism as their actions are in reality nothing more than crimes."

By the end of the war, at least twenty-six men were hanged at Breendonk. Another 157 died by firing squad at the camp. But it is possible that there were even more executions. Some prisoners remembered unusual incidents, such as the time a man was brought to the camp and taken around to the back, away from prisoners. Then they heard shots ring out. Others recalled a man hanged from the roof of the fort. But these deaths remain unsubstantiated.

———————

The executions did not stop the resistance. In the first four months of 1944, the military administration "acknowledged . . . 633 acts of sabotage against railway lines and 87 against the electrical grid."

As German losses mounted, the end of Breendonk was in sight.

THE MANY ENDINGS OF *AUFFANGLAGER* BREENDONK

May 1944–May 1945

From May to August 1944, the SS evacuated at least 964 prisoners from Breendonk in a series of transports to other concentration camps.

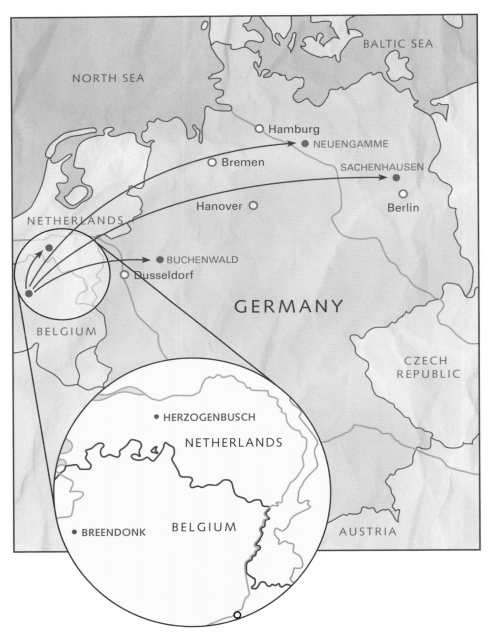

34

EVACUATING
BREENDONK

The main gate at Buchenwald today with its motto, Jedem das Seine
("To each what he deserves").

By April 1944, the population at Breendonk had reached an all-time high of about 660 prisoners. At the beginning of the month, rations were once again reduced; by its end, new cases of starvation edema were reported. A German senior medical officer requested that the rations be increased, but the SIPO-SD refused. Then, as rumors began to circulate about an Allied invasion to reclaim Belgium and the rest of Europe, the *Militärverwaltung* and the SIPO-SD asked for permission to begin transporting the prisoners of Breendonk to other concentration camps.

On May 6, 638 prisoners were sent to Buchenwald, a concentration camp near Weimar, Germany. This left only a skeleton crew of thirty-four prisoners at Breendonk, almost all of them tradesmen (carpenters, electricians, and tailors) with skills useful to the SS. During the next month, they were required to clean the camp and perform other routine maintenance. All the while, more prisoners who were resistance fighters arrived, until there were eighty-three inmates in residence.

On June 10, four days after the Allied landing on the Normandy beaches, the military administration feared a second Allied landing on the North Sea coast. Another sixty-four Breendonk prisoners were then transported, most to Buchenwald. Fewer than twenty prisoners remained at the camp, but this number slowly rose until there was another transport of fifty-three prisoners to Buchenwald on August 8.

Zugführer Valère De Vos was among those sent to Buchenwald that day. Unfortunately for De Vos, Buchenwald had many prisoners who had first been imprisoned at Breendonk. Word of his arrival spread quickly among the Belgian inmates.

By August 12, he was dead.

One Belgian prisoner, Bert Van Hoorick, described the events leading up to De Vos's death.

Van Hoorick saw De Vos standing in the middle of a tent at Buchenwald, surrounded by Breendonk prisoners. "I see him standing . . . eye to eye with those he had bullied, beaten, trampled. They insult him, shake their fists at him, spit and shout at him. . . . I see how panic overwhelms him. His eyes tell me he understands nothing. Here, it is still a concentration camp, he must be thinking, so where are the SS? But the SS does not deal with this kind of business. Here they are of no help. I walk away. . . . The next day, I learned that [De Vos] was beaten to death by those from Breendonk. At Buchenwald, there is no pity for the torturers."

It is not clear which Breendonk prisoners participated in his death; more than one claimed to be his murderer. One described, "I rushed him, and I kicked and kicked until he fell unconscious. I repeatedly hit his head on the ground."

Another told how a group of Breendonk prisoners took De Vos forcibly to a secluded spot and began to smother him with a pillow.

"Remember Breendonk, and go to Hell," the man told De Vos.

Next, "there was a great rumbling in his belly, and the smell of shit came out of his pants. Needless to say . . . [De Vos] understood . . . that he was going to kick the bucket."

No matter which version was true, De Vos did not succumb on the spot. He was taken to the infirmary, where he died, according to the official report, of bronchial pneumonia.

———

When British forces arrived at Breendonk on September 4, 1944, there were no prisoners to liberate, no SS to fight. The official ending of the camp occurred in silence. All remaining prisoners had been sent on two transports to other concentration camps:

263

When British troops arrived at Breendonk on September 4, 1944, they found piles of discarded uniforms.

one to Herzogenbusch in the Netherlands with 131 prisoners, and one to Neuengamme with 144 prisoners. Afterward, the SS had fled to Germany.

The camp was empty except for some resistance fighters who had decided to lock up a few brand-new prisoners: collaborators who had aided the Germans.

When Major Brice Somers of the British Royal Marines was taken to the fort on September 7, he was shocked by what he saw: "execution posts deeply chipped by bullets . . . torture chambers and dreadful crowded dormitories, all enclosed behind high walls." Inside the solitary-confinement cells, he saw collaborators who "seemed to be adequately fed and not mistreated, although some reached through the bars and plucked at my uniform, invoking their Mothers."

This new phase of Breendonk, called Breendonk II, lasted less than two months. Many collaborators were locked up in the fort, some placed there by police, some by resistance fighters. The prisoners—many of them innocent—were beaten and starved. Women suspected of collaborating with the Germans had their heads shaved and sometimes marked with swastikas.

Paul Lévy, who visited the fort during this time, was appalled with what he observed. "Collaborators are locked up and treated like we were treated by the Nazis," he said. "This inhumanity makes me sad."

That fall, the newly returned Belgian government tried to stop the abuses but failed. It was the British forces that brought about a change: on October 10, all prisoners were placed under British supervision and temporarily moved to the Dossin barracks—the former SS *Sammellager* in Mechelen. Some of the guards at Breendonk II were themselves arrested and jailed for sadistic behavior toward the prisoners.

Many collaborators were arrested after the Germans evacuated Belgium; some were sent to Breendonk.

Two months later, the Belgian government reopened Breendonk as an official internment center, supervised by officers and soldiers of the Belgian government. Incarcerated there would be "anyone suspected of collaborating with the enemy, at least sixteen years of age."

This time, there were no more abuses.

35

JOURNEY FROM MAUTHAUSEN

The Mauthausen concentration camp was known for its infamous stone quarries where prisoners were forced to work.

The evacuation of Breendonk was not the way the camp truly ended for most of its prisoners. If they had been transported to other concentration camps and had so far survived, they had to wait until the spring of 1945 for freedom. For them, Breendonk had been only the beginning of their concentration camp experience. And every one of the prisoners had his or her own unique story.

Life at these other camps was difficult, made harder by the terrible physical condition in which the prisoners had arrived. Of the 3,590 identified prisoners held in Breendonk, almost half (1,741) died. Of these, 1,384 prisoners (1,360 men and 24 women) died in other concentration camps or prisons.

Jean Dubois.

Jean Dubois was transported from Breendonk to the Mauthausen concentration camp near Linz, Austria, on November 9, 1942. The trip took five days, during which time the 242 prisoners were locked in their train cars and deprived of food and water. When they reached their destination, they still had to walk six miles up a steep hill to the camp. Placed in quarantine for two weeks, they were taught the required commands and procedures for their new camp. Dubois recalled being told by the camp commandant that there was only one exit from the camp: "He pointed in the direction of the smoke coming from a chimney."

Only 12 of the 242 prisoners from that transport would survive Mauthausen; Jean Dubois was one of them.

On their first day of work, they were led to the quarry in an area directly below the camp. To reach it, prisoners had to descend a steep, uneven stone stairway with 168 steps. At the quarry, each prisoner was ordered to pick up a block of granite, each weighing between thirty and forty pounds. Then

Prisoners who worked in the quarry at the Mauthausen concentration camp were forced to climb the 168-step "Stairway of Death" carrying a heavy block of granite many times each day.

marching five across—in formation, in unison—they ascended the steps holding the granite blocks on their shoulders. The only shoes they had were wooden clogs that could easily slip on the stones in wet or icy weather. The prisoners on the outer edge of the steps had the most difficult position. If someone near them collapsed or stumbled, the others might fall onto them, pushing them into the abyss below. Many fell accidentally to their death. Others were also pushed to their death by the SS. Some even jumped willingly, to escape the oppressive brutality. The steps became known as the Stairway of Death.

When the prisoners reached their destination with the granite blocks, they had to turn around and march back down to the quarry and repeat the task over and over again, trying hard to survive. At night, Dubois sometimes heard the *Kapos,* the prisoner room leaders at Mauthausen, talk with each other, bragging about how many prisoners they had killed that day.

Dubois survived the steps and his work at the quarry, in large part because he was transferred a month later to a subcamp named Gusen I, where he was assigned to the blacksmith shop. After eight months, he was sent to Wiener-Neudorf, a subcamp just south of Vienna, where he made airplane engines for Messerschmitt, a German aircraft manufacturer. Because the factory was also a target of Allied bombings, many prisoners died in air raids, but Dubois survived. He also endured a forced hundred-mile march of two

The Gusen concentration camp after liberation.

thousand prisoners from Vienna to Mauthausen in February 1945; half of the men on that march died or were killed when they could not keep up. Dubois survived one more subcamp of Mauthausen, Gusen II, where he assembled airplane wings. About 200,000 prisoners passed through Mauthausen during the war; at least half of them did not survive.

By the end of April 1945, Dubois and the other prisoners at Gusen II could tell that the Germans were losing the war, but they did not know when they would be liberated. Finally, on May 2, when they saw some villagers hanging white flags outside their windows, they realized that the war was over. Still, it took a few more days before American troops reached the subcamp. A few SS were still there, guarding the prisoners. One, in a watchtower, began to shoot at the Americans and was quickly killed by return fire. Other SS tried to surrender, "running with their hands in the air, but they were immediately cut down by a hail of bullets."

Although Dubois was liberated, he was not free to leave the camp. The Americans warned the former prisoners that the SS were still in the vicinity and might kill them. But Dubois had had enough. After they found a loaded revolver that they could use to protect themselves, he and a French prisoner decided to escape from their liberators. They cut through the barbed wire and headed back home—even if that meant walking six hundred miles. Dressed in their filthy prison uniforms, they frightened most people they encountered.

Prisoners who survived Mauthausen were guarded inside the camp after liberation by American soldiers.

The public had been told that the prisoners of Mauthausen were terrible criminals.

The first night of their journey, as they searched for a place to stay, a woman whose husband had been arrested during the war allowed them to stay in her house. Dubois and his friend were able to wash themselves with warm water and soap. The woman even laundered their clothes and gave them a bowl of stew for dinner. When it was time for bed, she placed a double mattress on the floor of her living room. That night, for the first time in almost three years, Jean Dubois slept on clean sheets. The feeling was indescribable.

Eventually, he and his friend were flown to northern France, where they went their separate ways. In Liège, Dubois was met by his parents, great-aunts and -uncles, and cousins. By the time he arrived in his small village near Genk, the main street had been decorated and the local men dressed in their blue work overalls formed an honor guard for him.

That was how Breendonk—and Mauthausen and many of its subcamps—ended for Jean Dubois on May 22, 1945.

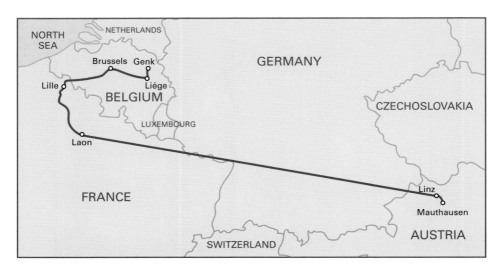

Jean Dubois traveled about a thousand miles to reach his home near Genk, Belgium, once he was liberated from Mauthausen-Gusen.

36

END OF THE SUPERMEN

Ernest Landau was forced to help build this airplane factory shortly before he was liberated; only its ruins remain today.

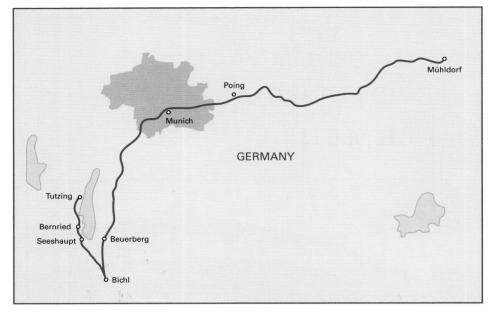

Ernest Landau survived a 110-mile train ride before he was liberated by American troops outside Tutzing, Germany.

In April 1943, Ernest Landau, one of Breendonk's early prisoners, was sent to Auschwitz-Birkenau on Transport XX from the SS *Sammellager* in Mechelen. Upon arrival, he was assigned to the Monowitz subcamp, a huge factory complex where the prisoners were slave laborers. He worked there for almost six months before he was transferred to a series of other camps. Over the next eighteen months, he was sent to a concentration camp in Warsaw, Poland; to Dachau concentration camp near Munich, Germany; and then to two of its subcamps, Allach and Mühldorf-Mettenheim. At Mühldorf, his final camp, he was forced to help build an airplane factory for Messerschmitt.

By the time the Allied forces were closing in on Munich, Landau and about 3,600 of his fellow prisoners, almost all of them Jews, were evacuated onto a hundred-car freight train guarded by a small artillery cannon on one flatbed car. The

train moved so sporadically, sometimes standing on a sid-
ing for hours, that it took about thirty-six hours to travel forty
miles to Poing, a village east of Munich. There, prisoners were
mistakenly told that the war was over; many left the train and
began to look for food. But the war had not ended, and other
SS in the village rounded up the prisoners. At least fifty were
killed in the melee and another two hundred injured as they
were herded back onto the train.

The train pushed on, this time to Munich, where it was
divided in half. The original train was so long and heavy that
it would not be able to reach its unspecified destination in the
Bavarian Alps. Train 1 carried Ernest Landau and 1,600 other
prisoners, while Train 2 held about 2,000.

On April 29, Landau's train reached Beuerberg, some
forty miles south of Munich, where it was spotted by American
bombers. Because the rail line at Beuerberg was often used
to transport bombs from a nearby factory, the pilots mistook
the prisoners' train for the one with a military purpose. As
the planes dove down to bomb and strafe the train, the SS
guards ran for shelter in the nearby woods, leaving the
prisoners behind.

Hoping to stop the planes from striking again, some
prisoners climbed onto the cars and laid their blue and green
striped prison jackets on the roofs. When the planes made another pass, this time the pilots saw the jackets and flew on by.

Some sixty prisoners died in the attack, but the train
continued on its way, diverted from its destination in the Alps.
Both trains made their way around the southern shore of Lake
Starnberg to Seeshaupt. Train 1 traveled north until it reached
the small village of Bernried; Train 2 remained in Seeshaupt.

———

As night fell on May 1, 1945, Landau's train was going no far-
ther. Shaken by the air raid in Beuerberg, the SS was now

A railroad car of corpses was found by American troops after Train 2 reached its final destination in Seeshaupt.

205483

transformed. Under ordinary circumstances, they would have ordered the prisoners out of the train cars and into line for an *Appell,* but they were no longer interested in counting them. The SS—these Nazi supermen, as Landau called them—appeared frightened. They allowed the prisoners to open the doors of their freight cars, to walk around, to drink water, and to engage them in conversation. Even guards who had been violent a few days earlier had softened. Landau took this as a sign that the Germans realized the war was lost.

Still, Landau wondered if they would kill all the prisoners or simply abandon them. By that time, many of the prisoners had not eaten for days.

They lay down in their train cars, waiting for morning. Near dawn, they heard a car engine; a large Mercedes with a Swiss flag attached to the hood was approaching. It held members of the Swiss consulate, who asked to speak to the person in charge. An SS sergeant soon arrived.

"But you're SS," one of the Swiss men complained. "I don't want to talk to you. I want to talk to one of the inmates."

Humiliated, the SS sergeant returned to his men and then sent the senior head prisoner, a kind of *Zugführer,* but one whom Landau considered to be "actually a decent guy."

The Swiss man was not impressed, since he had been selected by the SS.

"We want to talk to an inmate, an average inmate," the Swiss man insisted.

Some of the prisoners shoved Ernest Landau forward.

The chance to talk to the Swiss men was unusual for Landau; he had not talked to anyone who was not a prisoner or a guard in a prison camp for over four years.

"The liberators are near. You must have a little more patience," one of the Swiss men whispered to him. "Tell your people that . . . tomorrow morning at the latest you will be free."

They promised to return with food but warned Landau to be careful, not to trust the SS. When they were

Ernest Landau and the other prisoners of Train 1 were freed at this location near Bernried, Germany.

gone, Landau related the conversation to some of the other prisoners, who told and retold it to many other prisoners in other languages. "A feeling of resistance [was] suddenly awakened in us—a plan suddenly initiated."

Small groups of prisoners casually approached the SS guards, pretending to be friendly, engaging them in conversation. Soon, the prisoners had surrounded the individual guards and overpowered them. They took their guns and ammunition, tied them up, and put them inside one of the train cars, guarded by an armed prisoner with instructions to shoot anyone who attempted to escape. One SS man, the only one who had a reputation for being brutal, was killed.

Later that day, the food arrived as promised, but the famished prisoners were so hungry that they swarmed toward it, knocking the soup kettles over so that no one got more than a spoonful. Fortunately, there was enough sliced bread to sustain them another day.

———

The next morning, the Americans arrived.

As Landau remembered, "Forgotten are hunger, weariness, and fear. Forgotten are the privations of the transport. We are free now, really free. We all run from the train. The American soldiers are surrounded, embraced, kissed, and raised upon our shoulders."

What the soldiers saw were "starved, liberated people, emaciated to skin and bones, almost skeletons."

Food was distributed, but there was work to do. The corpses of the dead, those who had died on the train en route to nowhere and those who had died in the air raid, had to be buried in a grave. The Americans radioed for clergymen; a religious ceremony had to be performed for the funeral.

Soon the train moved on to Tutzing, where arrangements had been made to bury the dead in a new cemetery. Two chaplains, one Christian and one Jewish, arrived with a two-sided altar. One side displayed a cross, the other side the Ten Commandments. Since most of the transported prisoners were Jewish, a Jewish funeral ceremony would be performed by the Jewish chaplain, who was an American rabbi. The men needed to cover their head when they prayed, but they had no yarmulkes or hats or even handkerchiefs. Instead, some put the striped jacket of their prison uniform on their head. Others simply covered their head with their hands. It was the best they could do in this difficult circumstance.

The dead from Train 1 were buried in a mass grave in a cemetery in Tutzing; in 1953, the bodies were exhumed and reburied in Dachau.

Then the surviving prisoners recited prayers beside the mass grave in what Landau called "the most moving religious service [he had] ever experienced."

———

This was how Breendonk—and the SS *Sammellager* in Mechelen, and Auschwitz, and Warsaw, and the Dachau subcamps—ended for Ernest Landau: he had survived not only one more day; he had survived the entire war. A group of starving, ordinary men with a simple plan had defeated supermen.

It was truly a moment to remember.

37

THE FINAL TRANSPORT FROM NEUENGAMME

The Neuengamme concentration camp near Hamburg, Germany.

But there was another ending to Breendonk.

From September 24, 1941, until April 1945, the lawyer and poet René Blieck was a prisoner at Neuengamme, sent there on the first transport from Breendonk in September 1941.

Little is known about his time at the camp. In December 1942, he wrote his wife, acknowledging her recent letter. Every line of her letter, Blieck told her, helped him recall the smell of their house, the sound of her and their son's voices, and the beauty of Belgium. He was still thinking poetic thoughts in Neuengamme, still writing poetry in his head and on scraps of paper.

After the war, another Neuengamme prisoner recalled that many times Blieck had rallied other prisoners, especially those from Belgium. Speaking French, Dutch, and German, he warned them that suffering "was man's greatest enemy." They needed to remain strong and unmoved by emotional

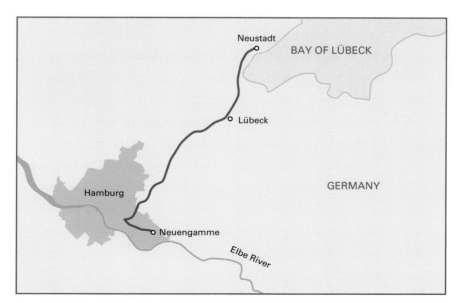

René Blieck and other prisoners from the Neuengamme concentration camp were transported to the Bay of Lübeck, where they were placed aboard two ships, the Cap Arcona *and the* Thielbeck.

and physical pain, he told them, because the more sensitive a person was, the more capacity he had to suffer.

His wife and other family members sent him occasional packages of food and clothing to nurture him. In one, she sent him an egg that had been secretly hollowed out. Inside was a small, rolled-up photo of his son, Pierre, whom he had last seen on the day of his arrest. Pierre was only four months old when the SIPO-SD took his father away.

Early on at the camp, Blieck was a concrete worker, a physically difficult job. By the beginning of 1943, he and another Belgian from Breendonk, Pierre de Tollenaere, found work in one of the factories on the grounds of the camp: the Jastram plant, which manufactured U-boats and torpedoes. The company from Hamburg had established a small factory in a shed at Neuengamme in April 1942. By 1943, there were more sheds and about 150 prisoners forced to work for the company.

How Blieck was able to change jobs is unexplained in existing camp documents. It would have been difficult for a laborer to arrange a move to a desk job, though. At the very least, Blieck and de Tollenaere would have been tested to make sure that their skills were satisfactory and would have received, perhaps, further training. Blieck worked in the Jastram office, while de Tollenaere worked on torpedo tube production. He must have visited the factory workers as often as he could, because another prisoner working there remembered Blieck vividly: as the prisoners went about their various jobs, Blieck—"in his wooden clogs looking miserable and yellowish"—recited poetry to them. As they listened, "his sprightly, humorous poems whirled through the room . . . spreading a good mood" among the workers.

The Jastram jobs were demanding, sometimes requiring prisoners to work seven days a week. As long as the prisoners were at work, though, they were supervised by more

René Blieck and Pierre de Tollenaere worked at the Jastram factory at Neuengamme.

lenient civilian employees, not SS guards. Factory workers at Neuengamme could also receive some additional food. But the moral tradeoff was difficult, since they knew that the work they did might prolong the war and even help the Germans to win. To counteract this, some resorted to careful but deliberate sabotage of their work.

In November 1944, Pierre de Tollenaere was accused of sabotage when a bad weld that he had made on a torpedo tube was discovered. Some prisoners believed that de Tollenaere was singled out for working too slowly, but he told others that he had made the bad weld on purpose. No matter what was true, when the camp commandant, Max Pauly, learned of the accusation, he interrogated de Tollenaere briefly, then ordered him to be hanged on the *Appell* grounds. The death was meant to serve as a warning for the other prisoners.

The afternoon before the execution, camp carpenters assembled a six-foot-tall gallows, stored in several pieces for the all-too-frequent hangings. Some inmates of Neuengamme, especially those who worked in the factories, where sabotage might be a temptation, would be lined up in rows and forced to watch. René Blieck would be among them.

The next day, Sunday, December 10, de Tollenaere was escorted to the gallows. An SS officer read a statement, as remembered by one prisoner who witnessed the event: "In the name of the *Reichsführer* SS, de Tollenaere will be hanged because of sabotage; he is condemned to death." Then two prisoners were ordered to place the noose around his neck. Others removed the board he was standing on, and he dropped through the trap some two feet. He was allowed to hang for five minutes before he was cut down and taken to the mortuary. The prisoners soon heard the sound of a single shot as the execution was completed.

René Blieck was devastated by his friend's death and wrote a poem about it that day. Then he memorized it and, as he had at Breendonk, taught it to some of his friends at Neuengamme.

———

On April 19, as part of the camp's evacuation plan, 10,000 Neuengamme prisoners were placed on board cattle cars, one hundred men crammed inside each, and transported north to Lübeck, a port on the Baltic Sea. Many of the prisoners were sick, and all were starving and dehydrated. At least three thousand died on the fifty-mile journey. From there, the surviving prisoners were marched twelve miles to the town of Neustadt, where most were herded aboard two ships, the *Cap Arcona* and the *Thielbeck,* which were anchored in the Bay of Lübeck. The Neuengamme prisoners, along with inmates from some other concentration camps, were packed into the holds, where drinking water, food, and medical attention were in short supply, even though some prisoners were dying of typhoid fever.

René Blieck was aboard one of these two ships.

The ships were not in good condition, and the plans for the prisoners were not known. After the war, conflicting testimony was given at a war crimes trial: one Nazi party official stated that under orders from Berlin, the prisoners were to be shipped to Sweden. The head of a Gestapo unit, however, maintained that the ships were to have been scuttled at sea, ensuring that all the prisoners would die.

Neither happened.

———

On May 3, 1945, with the war almost at an end and British troops closing in on Neustadt—three days after Hitler committed suicide in Berlin—the ships were attacked by the British Royal Air Force. Such an attack was not a complete surprise,

The wreckage of the Cap Arcona; *part of the ship drifted to shore and was finally dismantled in 1949.*

since German ships in the Baltic Sea had regularly transported troops.

The *Cap Arcona* was hit by two rockets initially. "The first smoke-trailing missile . . . landed between the first and second funnels. The next struck the third funnel and skidded along

In February 1950, the wreckage of the Thielbeck *was raised and towed to shore, where former prisoners greeted it with lowered flags.*

the Sports Deck. . . . In minutes, the entire upper third of the *Cap Arcona* was in flames. . . . At the waterline, a secondary explosion sent off . . . [blowing] a huge hole in the side, allowing water to pour in." By the time the attack was over, the RAF pilots from five Typhoon bombers had fired forty rockets at the *Cap Arcona,* and the ship was listing.

The *Thielbeck* was attacked next by four other Typhoon bombers; it sank twenty minutes later. Not long after, the *Cap Arcona* capsized. All but 450 people on the two ships perished when they were drowned, burned, or shot while trying to save themselves. The war ended in Europe five days later. René Blieck, who had endured so much, did not survive this final attack by Allied planes.

This was how Breendonk ended for him.

———

After the war, Ernest Gaillard, one of Blieck's surviving friends

from Neuengamme, met with the widows of Pierre de

Tollenaere and René Blieck. At this emotional meeting, Gaillard suddenly remembered the poem that Blieck had written the day that Pierre de Tollenaere had been executed. He had learned it by heart, and it suddenly came flooding back to him.

This last poem by Blieck, untitled, was written in the voice of Pierre de Tollenaere speaking to his wife after his death. But the poem could have been spoken by any Breendonk prisoner:

> Will you go slowly to a lonely place
> to kneel in silence and pray?
>
> Will you add my name to your prayer?
>
> And as you try to remember our past,
> will you forget your grief as your eyes wander up to the heavens
> where my still heart drifts?
>
> Come as the day fades.
> My heart will tremble again when I hear
> you murmur, "I love you still, my love."
>
> And one morning if bright spring
> makes pink buds bloom on a barren hill,
> bring them to your lips—my love,
>
> we can still exchange kisses
> beyond the grave.

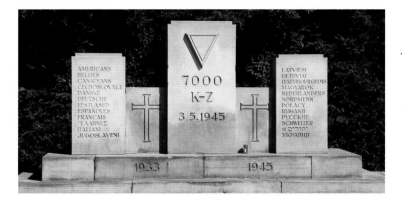

Today a memorial to the prisoners who died on the Cap Arcona *and the* Thielbeck *is situated along the shore of the Bay of Lübeck near Neustadt.*

1945–Present

38

THE WAR CRIMES
TRIALS

The war crimes trial in Mechelen.

By the end of 1944, as the final months of World War II were fought elsewhere in Europe, some former prisoners of Breendonk began to publish books about their experiences. These works, along with other reports, encouraged the search for the torturers and executioners of Breendonk so that they would be brought to justice. This included members of the German and Flemish SS, *Zugführers*, and civilian workers at the camp who had collaborated with the SS. Some were living openly, some had gone into hiding, and some had fled to Germany when the camp was evacuated. It took a while, but most were rooted out, some with the help of former Breendonk prisoners.

One of the most sought-after persons was Walter Obler, whom Paul Lévy desperately wanted to find. Convinced that Obler had returned to Vienna, Lévy encouraged Oskar

The accused war criminals were identified by numbered placards worn around their necks. Shown in this photograph are the former Breendonk Zugführers *Walter Obler (16), Sally Lewin (17), and Leo Schmandt (18).*

Hoffman, his old friend from Room 1, who had moved back to Vienna himself, to search for him. Hoffman agreed, although he knew that finding Obler in Vienna would be a daunting task.

One day, though, Hoffman by chance encountered Obler walking down the street. He followed him and discovered that Obler and his wife were living a simple life in a neighborhood where he was known as a "quiet and industrious workman who had spent some difficult years in concentration camps." His neighbors probably knew that he had been freed from the Mauthausen concentration camp in May 1945, after stays in both Auschwitz and Sachsenhausen, but none of them was aware of the time he had spent at Breendonk and the terror he had caused there. Hoffmann quickly contacted Belgian officials in Vienna. At eight o'clock on the evening of November 20, 1945, Obler was taken into custody.

Not long after, when Obler arrived back in Belgium to await trial, he met with Paul Lévy. He told Lévy that except for his wife and sister, all members of his family had been gassed in concentration camps. Lévy said that he "saw tears flow from Obler." He acknowledged that Obler was also "a victim of to-talitarianism and of violence," but he also knew that Obler had to pay for his own crimes.

––––––––

A series of trials was held for the men responsible for the crimes committed at Breendonk. One of the first was held in Mechelen, beginning on March 5, 1946, when twenty-three men—fourteen members of the Flemish SS, six former *Zugführers,* and three Belgian civilian workers at the camp— were prosecuted.

During the five-week trial, the accused were seated in the courtroom, each wearing a large number on a sign around his neck. Now, like the Breendonk prisoners they abused, they

Fernand Wyss.

*Ernest Landau
was among the
witnesses to testify
at the trial.*

were identified by number: Wyss (1), Obler (16), Lewin (17), and
Schmandt (18). Although Richard De Bodt had not been found
and Valère De Vos had been killed at Buchenwald, both were
still charged and tried in absentia.

Some 449 witnesses were called to testify. Many spoke
against Wyss. Marguerite Paquet told the court that despite his

protests to the contrary, Wyss was in the bunker all seven times that she was tortured and that he "extinguished his cigarette on her back." She had the scars to prove her accusation.

Ernest Landau testified about the abuses of the Flemish SS and *Zugführer* Obler. He also recalled the last day of Israel Neumann as he languished in the *Revier*, unable to eat. Neumann's wife, Eleonore Sabathova, also offered testimony. In March 1941, five months after her husband was arrested, she was notified that she could send him food packages once a month. Three months later, she was informed that Neumann was being punished and was no longer allowed to receive packages. Finally, on July 26, she received a letter telling

The former Zugführer *Walter Obler defended himself on the witness stand.*

her that her husband had died two days earlier "after a short illness."

Lawyers offered a defense of the accused from April 10 through April 12. During this time, Obler took the stand and denied that he had ever asked a prisoner for money or jewelry.

When asked about the charges of brutality and murder against him, he told the courtroom, through tears, "I still do not understand how I could have been so cruel. I truly do not know how."

————

On May 7, 1946, the court announced its verdict. Only one of the twenty-three accused was acquitted, a former *Zugführer* named Henri Van Borm. Six others were given prison terms: four received life sentences, one was given twenty years, and the former *Zugführer* Leo Schmandt received fifteen years.

The remaining sixteen men, including the absent De Bodt and De Vos, were sentenced to death. The court found that Wyss was responsible for the death of sixteen prisoners and the abuse of 167 others; De Bodt for ten deaths and the abuse of 125 prisoners; Obler for ten deaths and the abuse of sixteen prisoners; and De Vos for two deaths and the abuse of nineteen prisoners.

Most of the prisoners appealed their verdict. To reduce the sentence of his client, the lawyer for *Zugführer* Sally Lewin claimed that he was not responsible for any crimes because he had to obey the commands of SS-Lieutenant Prauss. Lewin was found guilty in the death of eight prisoners, including Hirsz Swirski, but his lawyer argued that he had only thrown water onto Swirski to help revive him, not to kill him. Swirski, the lawyer insisted, died of a brain hemorrhage, not from anything Lewin did. He asked for the death sentence to be removed. The court, however, upheld all of the sentences.

One final chance remained for the condemned men; they could request a government pardon. In the end, two Flemish SS guards had their death sentences commuted to life in prison. For the others, the proceedings were over.

The Belgian public called for the executions to be held

Walter Obler on his way to the courtroom to learn the verdict.

at Breendonk, but the government opposed this idea: "We do not practice executions in the places where the Germans themselves have performed them," one official explained. Another solution had to be found.

————

After the war, almost 2,500 people were convicted of collaboration with the Germans in Belgium and sentenced to death. Only 242 of these sentences, however, were carried out. The twelve sentenced to die for their crimes at Breendonk were among them.

On April 12, 1947, the twelve men were scheduled to die by firing squad. Ten of the men, including Obler and Lewin, were locked up in a prison in Mechelen. Wyss was incarcerated in the Begijnenstraat prison in Antwerp, where Charlotte Hamburger and Louis De Houwer were jailed for a time. The twelfth man was imprisoned in Namur, in southern Belgium.

Early that morning the ten men were taken by car to the execution place, a barrack next to the former SS *Sammellager* in Mechelen. About five hundred people were in attendance, including Louis Bamps, the bar owner from Mechelen, who sat in a wheelchair that morning because of the terrible crippling injuries he had suffered after being repeatedly tortured at Breendonk.

The men would be executed in two groups, five at a time. Sixty police officers divided into five platoons of twelve took their positions ten paces from the posts. Each condemned man would face twelve rifles. One rifle for each platoon, though, was loaded with blanks, so that none of the officers would know if his gun had live ammunition.

Paul Lévy was outspoken in his belief that the accused criminals should not be executed.

Obler was in the first group of five prisoners. Each man had a priest or minister, or in the case of Obler, a rabbi, to give them a final blessing or comfort; Obler waved the rabbi away. The men were tied to the posts with their backs to the firing squad. As collaborators with the Germans, they were not entitled to an honorable death; they were to be shot in the back. When the squad was ordered to shoot, two men died immediately; three others had to be finished with a final shot. But Obler did not die easily; four or five additional bullets were reportedly needed to kill him.

The bodies were removed from the posts, placed in coffins, and carried from the field. Then the final five, which included Sally Lewin, were brought to the field. Lewin was killed as he recited a Jewish prayer.

In Antwerp, at the same time the eleventh man was executed in Namur, Fernand Wyss was taken to the grounds of an old military bakery and executed. Afterward, a doctor checked the body and announced that "ten bullets hit the convicted man's heart."

39

THE FINAL DEATH

Philipp Schmitt was taken to Breendonk shortly after his arrest in 1944. Paul Lévy is in the background on the right.

The government of Belgium had much less luck in locating and trying members of the German SS.

The first and the easiest to be found was former SS-Major Philipp Schmitt. After he left Breendonk in 1943, he was transferred to Denmark, where he was assigned the task of searching for Danish resistance fighters. From there, he was sent to Roermond in the Netherlands. When the war ended, he was arrested and jailed in Rotterdam, where no one suspected his true identity as the former commandant of Breendonk.

On November 20, 1945, the same day that Obler was arrested, Schmitt was recognized at the Rotterdam prison and returned to Belgium, accompanied by a team that included Paul Lévy. At Lévy's request, Schmitt was taken back to Fort Breendonk, where the two men were greeted by a number of former prisoners. Although they treated Schmitt respectfully, Lévy let him know that he would soon face justice. Schmitt was escorted slowly through the camp. He walked with a cane now, having been wounded in the Netherlands by American artillery fire, and said nothing to his former prisoners.

"Take off your hat," one former prisoner finally ordered. Breendonk prisoners had always been punished for failing to remove their hats.

"For fifteen years," another told him, "you have followed a false belief."

"I must reeducate myself" was all that Schmitt replied.

Then he was locked up in one of the solitary-confinement cells for two days. Asked how he felt to be placed in a cell, he replied, "Oh, I can stand it all right. I'm an SS officer."

For almost four years, Schmitt was detained in the Begijnenstraat prison in Antwerp. He could not be tried at that time, since Belgian law had no provision for prosecuting citizens of another country for war crimes. He was questioned repeatedly but did not offer much information. In time, the law was amended.

Philipp Schmitt's trial began on August 2, 1949. He was charged with eighty-three deaths at Breendonk. During the trial, the judges accompanied Schmitt on a visit to the camp. In the bunker, which the SS had dismantled before the final evacuation, Schmitt expressed displeasure with the way the room had been recreated.

During his trial, Philipp Schmitt returned to Breendonk.

"As far as I know, this pulley was attached to another place and these sharp wooden blocks were neither so high nor so sharp," he told the judges.

Many former prisoners testified against him.

On the stand himself, he was asked by the president of the tribunal, "How is it that your dog has attacked and injured so many prisoners?"

"Excuse me?" he replied. "You can say what you want,

but it happened only twice. . . . Each time it was after an escape attempt. You should also know that the prisoners would mistreat my poor dog."

"Don't you find it odd that at least seventy-four prisoners reported having been bitten by your dog or seeing someone bitten?" the president continued.

"I cannot explain it to you," Schmitt said.

"Don't you think it serious that the prisoners received so many beatings?"

"Oh! That depends on what you mean by beatings. If a prisoner is disobedient, you are obliged to intervene."

"Can you at least tell me what sanctions you took when your subordinates committed these abuses?"

Schmitt could not give an answer.

On November 25, 1949, Schmitt was found guilty "of 57 murders, of the illegal arrest of 35 Jews, and of instigating (and executing) numerous physical attacks on inmates." He was sentenced to death.

Wilfried Hallemans, the head prosecutor, charged Schmitt with his crimes.

On August 8, 1950, he was taken to the same location where Wyss had faced the firing squad. At six in the morning, he refused to be blindfolded and was shot, the only Nazi war criminal executed in Belgium. In fact, his was the last execution ever held in the country.

———————

As for the other German SS officers, the former SS lieutenants Prauss and Kantschuster were never found, though it was rumored that Prauss died in a bunker on April 19, 1945, during the final assault on Berlin. Schmitt's replacement as commandant, Karl Schönwetter, also disappeared. A few lower-level members of the SS received prison terms, but no one else was sentenced to death.

The next year, on July 9, 1951, the Flemish SS Richard De Bodt was finally captured. Although he had been sentenced to death at the 1946 Mechelen trial, a government official now saw fit to commute his sentence to life in prison with hard labor, a move that angered the Belgian public. Various demonstrations were held throughout the country; flags were lowered to half mast in protest; and the teachers' union in Antwerp refused "to comply with the Government request to commemorate in schools the anniversary of the liberation of Belgium on Sept. 8 in view of what they called the Government's unpatriotic acts." In the end, the official responsible for the decision resigned, but his action could not be undone.

De Bodt's time in prison was anything but hard labor; it was quiet and filled with leisurely activities such as reading and drawing. Still an ardent Nazi, he received a Christmas package from former SS friends every year. Once, when he was confronted by a former Breendonk prisoner, De Bodt "expressed absolutely no regrets" about his past. He died in prison, suffering badly from diabetes, on January 3, 1975.

40

BREENDONK TODAY

"For four long years, Breendonk was the pride of the Gestapo.
Today it's the pride of free men." —Paul Lévy

*Today visitors are directed to the entrance of Breendonk
with this sign.*

I n 1947, the former military fortress officially became the National Memorial Fort Breendonk, a museum that keeps alive the memory of everything that took place there.

After the war, there was much misinformation about the camp. Some reports talked of its gas chambers, of the bodies of the victims being cremated and not buried, of multiple torture rooms, and much more. Today the memorial clarifies what actually happened at the camp by allowing visitors to walk through its rooms, which are filled with exhibits about the prisoners and their tormentors.

Almost all the original camp still exists. As you turn in to the parking lot, you can even see the now-deserted house of Mr. and Mrs. Verdickt opposite the main entrance, though most visitors have no idea what happened there; they have never heard of *Le Flitser*.

After a brief stop in the visitors' center, you cross a short

A propaganda photograph of the SS greets visitors as they enter the fort today.

wooden bridge over the moat to reach the entry to the fort. Immediately, you are hit in the face by the blast of cool wind that barrels through the mouth of the entrance tunnel. Stepping inside, standing on uneven cobblestones, you are confronted with the overwhelming darkness—visual and emotional—of the former fort. It is not, even as a memorial, a friendly place. It demands that you pay your respects.

Your first stop on the self-guided tour is the canteen, where the photographs of the twelve men from Senzeilles

The inaccurate death certificates of some Breendonk prisoners are exhibited in the former kitchen.

are featured. This is where they were tried and sentenced to death. Next, you move on to the kitchen, with its bright yellow tile work. Here, photographs of the early death certificates are blown up in a huge display, so you can see that so many men died of "natural causes" after having been beaten, starved, and tortured. This is the room where Adrien Henderickx and seven others were forced to drink boiling soup after they were found stealing food from the pigsty. At the far end of the room is a photo of Israel Neumann snapped by the propaganda photographer, as he struggled to carry a pot of soup.

From the kitchen, you step outside into the west court-yard, where so many prisoners had to face the wall upon their arrival. In the center is a small brick building that served as the SS office. Today it exhibits the photographs of the Flemish SS, including Fernand Wyss and Richard De Bodt.

Next, you are directed across the entrance tunnel to the east courtyard, where *Appell* took place. This is where the corpses of Mozes Louft and Isaak Trost were displayed for all to see. Nearby is all that remains of the original toilets: one small building with four partial stalls, each with a hole in the floor. The space is so narrow that a prisoner would have had to back up into it.

Inside again, you enter the long barracks hallway. In Room 1, where the first prisoners were housed beginning in the fall of 1940, photographs of Walter Obler and his wife, Maria Skamene, are exhibited. In Rooms 8 and 9, you observe the sixteen solitary-confinement cells where prisoners such as Jose Cornet were detained for long periods of time. In Rooms 13 and 14, you come across the *Revier*. This is where Israel Neumann—and so many others—died. Across the hall, you notice the morgue, its entrance blocked by iron bars; inside are a few coffins.

As you turn the corner and begin to head down another hall, one room down a narrow corridor on the left draws your attention. The bunker—still oppressive and chilling—awaits you there. The space alone is terrifying; the memory of what hap-pened to Hans Mayer or Marguerite Paquet is unbearable.

After you pass the Jewish barracks, you step back outside and walk around the fort to the execution ground with its ten wooden posts and three-position gallows. A nearby plaque gives the names of everyone who was known to have been

Photographs of Walter Obler and Maria Skamene are displayed in Room 1.

executed there. You can find the names of André Bertulot, Louis De Houwer, Arnaud Fraiteur, Maurice Raskin, Josef Suy, and Georges Van Wassenhove, among all the others.

Next, you reenter the east courtyard and pass by the stables where the horses' names are still on signs above their stalls. You visit the tailoring workshop of Herszel Frydman and his sons and walk through the original six windowless solitary-confinement cells. Among the last rooms is a memorial that honors the victims of all Nazi concentration camps. There the names of all known Breendonk prisoners are displayed on the wall.

As you finish your tour, you realize that you are walking through the architecture of a nightmare. You have walked in the footsteps of those who survived or those who died here or elsewhere during the war. You have visited a place where men and women suffered.

You remind yourself that you are in a different time and place. You are, you hope, in a different world.

Today the names of the prisoners from Breendonk are posted on the walls of the Memorial Room.

But a tour of Breendonk does not end there.

It ends in the villages and cities of Belgium, Germany, and Austria to which some surviving prisoners returned. It ends in other concentration camps where Breendonk prisoners, like Jean Dubois, were freed at the end of the war. It ends on the railroad tracks near Bernried where Ernest Landau was liberated.

But it also ends at the site of the Tir National in Schaerbeek, where the bodies of many of the men executed at Breendonk have now been interred under a field of crosses and Stars of David.

It ends in the concentration camps of Buchenwald, Dachau, Mauthausen, and Sachsenhausen, among many others, where the transported prisoners of Breendonk died. It ends in Auschwitz-Birkenau, where over 25,000 Jews living in Belgium were sent and only 1,240 survived. It ends for at least one Breendonk prisoner in the hold of the *Thielbeck* or the *Cap Arcona*.

And it ends in a small cemetery in Kraainem, an eastern suburb of Brussels, some twenty miles from Breendonk, where the bodies of twenty-three Jews, including Ludwig Juliusberger, Josef Rormann, Hugo Schönagel, Oscar Beck, and Wolf Hartlooper, who were murdered at the camp, are now buried. The simple monument above them reads TO OUR MARTYRS 1940–1945 in three languages: Dutch, French, and Hebrew.

Here, you will also find Israel Neumann's final resting place, a long way from his birthplace in Poland, a long way from his family's new home in New York.

Here, you will reflect on what happened to him.

Here, you will decide to never forget him and the other prisoners of Breendonk.

AFTERWORD

WHAT HAPPENED TO SOME BREENDONK PRISONERS AND THEIR FAMILIES

ALTER BRÉZINER: The *schochet* who was drawn twice by Jacques Ochs was a devout Jew, who during Passover week at Breendonk gave his bread to other prisoners. He was released from the camp in early 1942 and returned home to his wife and six children in Antwerp. In August that year, his three youngest daughters (Chaja, Brucha, and Ester) responded to the *Arbeitseinsatzbefehl* and were sent to Auschwitz-Birkenau on Transport VI. During the third Antwerp razzia, Bréziner, his wife, Chana, their daughter Rywka, and her husband, David, were arrested. On September 15,

The Bréziner family, c. 1920.

all four were placed on Transport X. Bréziner and his wife, his four daughters, and his son-in-law were murdered at Auschwitz. Only his two sons, Chaim and Abraham, avoided deportation and survived.

JOSE CORNET: After three months at Breendonk, Cornet was sent to two other Belgium prisons before he was transported to a succession of three concentration camps. He was liberated from Dachau on April 29, 1945.

RENÉ DILLEN: After his deportation to Neuengamme concentration camp in September 1941, Dillen was later sent first to the Mauthausen concentration camp near Linz, Austria, and then to the Gusen subcamp. He died there on April 21, 1943.

SCHYJA DOLINGER: When Dolinger's wife, Perla Sturm recte Frei, and their daughter, Edith, reported to SS-*Sammellager* Mechelen with an *Arbeitseinsatzbefehl*, they were deported to Auschwitz-Birkenau on Transport VI. Earlier, his sister, Rosalie, and her husband, Moses Grun, had arrived at the *Sammellager* with work orders; they were deported on Transport II. His brother, Israel, Israel's wife, Sara Wolf, and their children, Anne and Marcel, were arrested during the first Antwerp razzia and were placed on Transport V. None of them survived.

Perla Sturm recte Frei.

ABRAHAM FELDBERG: After his release in November 1941, Feldberg went into hiding and survived.

NACHMAN FELTSCHER: Feltscher's wife, Grete Brand, was arrested and placed on Transport II like Feltscher himself, although they were not assigned to the same railroad car. Neither survived.

JEAN FRANKLEMON: One of the three men who stopped Transport XX, Franklemon was eventually sentenced to six years' imprisonment by the Nazis and transferred first to the Sonnenburg concentration camp in April 1944, then to Sachsenhausen concentration camp. He was liberated from Sachsenhausen at the end of the war and lived in Germany where he worked as a professional musician. He died in 1977.

Grete Brand.

SACHA FRENKEL: Frenkel's wife, Rucha Schultz, was deported on Transport XIV and did not survive.

Rucha Schultz.

THE FRYDMAN FAMILY: Although Commandant Schmitt told Herszel Frydman and his three sons that they would be freed, only the sons were liberated in January 1942. They went into hiding and survived the war. Schmitt later sent Herszel to SS-*Sammellager* Mechelen, where he was deported on Transport IV. He did not survive.

WILLY GIERSCH: Released from Breendonk in February 1941, he was rearrested by the end of the year and jailed in a series of prisons. In July 1942, he arrived at the Sachsenhausen concentration camp, where he was tortured and imprisoned for the rest of the war. After liberation, he was arrested and returned to Belgium, where he was sentenced to fifteen years in jail. He was released in 1951, without serving his complete sentence, and allowed to return to Germany.

FISHEL HOROWITZ: Horowitz and his wife, Rosa Reisla, were assigned to Transport IX. Reisla was taken to Auschwitz-Birkenau, but Horowitz was removed from the train at Cosel, Poland, along with other men aged fifty-five and younger and sent to a labor camp, the first of six he was assigned to. He was liberated from Buchenwald in April 1945. His wife did not survive.

Margot Lewin.

JÜRGEN JACOBSOHN: After he left Breendonk in November 1941, Jacobsohn went home to his Brussels suburb, where he lived with his wife, Margot Lewin, and his mother, Lucie Freymann. All three were arrested in November 1943, taken to SS-*Sammellager* Mechelen, and sent to Auschwitz-Birkenau on Transport XXIII in January 1944. None of them survived.

JACOB KIPER: Kiper's wife, Laja Gewelbe, was deported on Transport XIII and did not survive; their daughter, Cécile, escaped deportation.

PHILIPPE LAMM: By the time he was murdered by the moat in January 1943, Lamm's stepmother, Magda Schwarz, and his sister, Marguerite, had already been sent to Auschwitz-Birkenau. His stepmother had responded to the *Arbeitseinsatzbefehl* and was deported on Transport II; his sister was sent on Transport XXIIB; neither survived. His brother, Richard, and Richard's Catholic wife, Yvonne Dewailly, were not deported.

Laja Gewelbe and Cécile Kiper.

ERNEST LANDAU: Liberated by American troops near Tutzing, Germany, Landau helped organize a camp for displaced persons in Feldafing, Germany, after the war. A few weeks after liberation, he married a woman who had also been a prisoner at the camp. He and his family resided in Germany, where he worked as a journalist for most of his life. He died in 2000.

PAUL LÉVY: Released from Breendonk on November 20, 1941, Lévy subsequently escaped to England, where he reported on the war, including the conditions at Breendonk, for the BBC. After the war, he covered the liberation of the Dachau concentration camp near Munich and the Belgian war crime trials in Mechelen. He died on August 16, 2002.

ALINE LOITZANSKI: Loitzanski was sent to Auschwitz-Birkenau on Transport V. She did not survive.

MOZES LOUFT: After his death, his wife, Rajzla Bicher, went to SS-*Sammellager* Mechelen with an *Arbeitseinsatzbefehl* and was deported on Transport I to Auschwitz-Birkenau. She did not survive.

Rajzla Bicher.

ROBERT MAISTRIAU: One of the three men who stopped Transport XX, Maistriau continued to work with the Belgian resistance until he was arrested in March 1944 and sent to Breendonk. Eventually, he was transported to Buchenwald and transferred to a series of three camps. He was liberated at Bergen-Belsen. He died in Belgium on September 26, 2008.

HANS MAYER: Transferred to SS-*Sammellager* Mechelen in February 1943, he was sent to Auschwitz-Birkenau on Transport XXIII. There, he was selected to perform difficult physical labor but was moved to a clerk's job six months later because of his writing skills. When Auschwitz was evacuated in January 1945, he was transferred to a succession of three camps before he was liberated in Bergen-Belsen. After the war, he returned to Belgium, where he changed his name to Jean Améry (an anagram of Mayer) to disavow his Germanic origins. He was the author of many books, including one about his torture in Breendonk. He committed suicide in 1978.

ISRAEL NEUMANN FAMILY: Once they arrived in New York City in 1921, the renamed Newman family lived in Brooklyn, first at 570 Van Siclen Street, then at 1617 President Avenue. Israel's father, Simon, was a Hebrew teacher, according to 1925 census records. He died in the late 1930s. Sylvia, a hairdresser, became the head of the family, which consisted by then only of her mother and her brother Milton. All three became naturalized United States citizens, and Milton joined the U.S. Coast Guard in June 1942; his enlistment papers indicated that he attended only grammar school and worked as a hatmaker. Another son, Jacob, preceded his family to New York and in 1921 lived at 2074 Mapes Avenue in the Bronx.

HERZ NISENHOLZ: The first person to escape from Breendonk, Nisenholz reportedly made his way to Switzerland and dropped out of sight.

JACQUES OCHS: Although he was released from Breendonk, he was later rearrested along with his sister, Hedwig, and sent to SS-*Sammellager* Mechelen. Their status as Jews was questioned long enough that they were able to avoid deportation to Auschwitz-Birkenau. They were freed on September 4, 1944.

ISRAEL ROSENGARTEN: Arrested in July 1941, Rosengarten was eventually transported to a labor camp in Poland and survived the war. His mother, Grine Brüh, and his three brothers, Leopold, Isi, and Henry, were arrested during the second Antwerp razzia and deported on Transport VII; they did not survive. His father, David, was placed on Transport XVIII and also did not survive.

ELEONORE SABATHOVA: After her husband, Israel Neumann, was sent to Breendonk, Sabathova continued to live in Antwerp. When Jews were required to sign the Jewish Register, she did so on December 20, 1940. A year later, she was hidden in a tuberculosis sanatorium, where she remained safely for the duration of the war.

Eleonore Sabathova.

ISRAEL STEINBERG: Steinberg was released from prison on October 30, 1946, and deported to Poland. From that date until at least August 1960, when he disappeared from the record, he was arrested twice each in Austria and Italy, where he was jailed for nine months and twelve months respectively. But he also continued to return to Belgium, where he was arrested six more times and served a total of eighteen months in prison. His crimes ranged

Israel Steinberg.

from pickpocketing to having false identification papers. He continued to claim that his wife and five children, ranging in age from nine to eighteen, had been shot by the Nazis in 1942. There is no way to know if this was true.

ELJASZ SWIRSKI: Sometime after his brother Hirsz's murder, Eljasz was freed from Breendonk and arrested again on August 14, 1942. Taken to SS-*Sammellager* Mechelen, he was deported on Transport XVII. He was selected for work at Auschwitz and given registration number 72861. He was eventually transferred to Golleschau, a slave-labor subcamp of Auschwitz. His parents, Morduch Swirski and Pesa Bursztejn, and his sister, Cypora, were arrested on October 12, 1942, and placed on Transport XIV. Swirski, his parents, and his sister did not survive.

MOZES WEISSBART: Deported on Transport II, he did not survive.

NUSEM ZYBENBERG: Before he was murdered by the moat at Breendonk on January 27, 1943, his family had already been deported. His oldest daughter, Anna, responding to the *Arbeitseinsatzbefehl,* arrived at SS-*Sammellager* Mechelen on August 1, 1942, where she was placed on Transport II. His wife, Dwojra Kaner, and his other three children, Rosa, Helena, and Bernard, were arrested during the second Antwerp razzia in August 1942, and sent to Auschwitz-Birkenau on Transport VII. Neither his wife nor his children survived.

Dwojra Kaner.

Rosa Zybenberg.

Anna Zybenberg.

APPENDIX 1

MAIN DEPORTATIONS FROM *AUFFANGLAGER* BREENDONK

Departure Date	Destination	Number of Prisoners	Number of Survivors
September 22, 1941	Neuengamme	105	21
May 8, 1942	Mauthausen	120	16
July 5, 1942	Mauthausen	24	9
September 30, 1942	Mauthausen	11	0
November 9, 1942	Mauthausen	238	37
February 9, 1944	Herzogenbusch	56	40
February 29, 1944	Herzogenbusch	49	25
May 6, 1944	Buchenwald	638	361
August 8, 1944	Buchenwald	56	40
August 30, 1944	Neuengamme	149	32
August 30, 1944	Sachsenhausen	131	62

APPENDIX 2

DEPORTATIONS FROM SS-*SAMMELLAGER* MECHELEN

Transport Number	Departure Date	Number of Prisoners	Number of Survivors
I	August 4, 1942	999	9
II	August 11, 1942	999	3
III	August 15, 1942	1,000	5
IV	August 18, 1942	1,000	0
V	August 25, 1942	996	27
VI*	August 29, 1942	1,000	35
VII*	September 1, 1942	1,000	15
VIII	September 8, 1942	1,000	34
IX*	September 12, 1942	1,000	30
X	September 15, 1942	1,047	25
XI	September 26, 1942	1,741	31
XII*	October 10, 1942	1,000	28
XIII*	October 10, 1942	681	26
XIV	October 24, 1942	998	15
XV	October 24, 1942	477	26
XVI	October 31, 1942	999	49
XVII	October 31, 1942	938	37
XVIII	January 15, 1943	997	4
IXX	January 15, 1943	627	8
XX	April 19, 1943	1,631	151
XXI	July 31, 1943	1,563	43
XXIIA	September 20, 1943	639	32
XXIIB	September 20, 1943	794	19
XXIII**	January 15, 1944	659	99
XXIV	April 4, 1944	626	147
XXV	May 19, 1944	508	134
XXVI	July 31, 1944	563	186

*Train stopped in Cosel, Poland (sixty miles from Auschwitz), where men and boys who could work were discharged to a labor camp. Approximately 1,280 men and older boys were taken from the trains at Cosel.

**An additional transport, designated by the letter Z for the German word *Zigeuner,* or Gypsy, departed the same day as Transport XXIII, carrying 351 Romany to Auschwitz-Birkenau; only 32 survived.

QUOTATION SOURCES

INTRODUCTION
1 "had no gas chambers . . .": Peeraer, "'t Gruwelkamp Breendonk, Doorleefde Nachtmerries."

"would prefer to spend": Klieger, "Un jour je te tuerai, cochon!," 1.

2 "was widely known . . .": Fulbrook, *A Small Town Near Auschwitz*, 215.

3 "which made it": [Lévy], "Breendonk Concentration Camp," National Memorial Fort Breendonk Archive, Item 138, 2.

"for no plausible reason": Hoyaux, *32 mois sous la matraque des S.S.*, 42.

1. THE ARREST OF ISRAEL NEUMANN
10 "deformed or crippled": List or Manifest of Alien Passengers for the United States Immigration Officer at Port of Arrival, SS *Roussillon*, ellisisland.org, 1 February 1921, pp. 289–90, line 10.

12 "I was hungry": National Archives of Belgium, Section 5, "Archives contemporaines," Israel Neumann, Bestuurlijke Akte, 8 May 1929.

"small size, dark eyes . . .": National Archives of Belgium, Section 5, "Archives contemporaines," Israel Neumann, Bulletin central de signalements, 21 October 1940.

13 "vomited": Fischer, *L'enfer de Breendonck*, 27.

2. BUILDING BREENDONK
19 "considered a threat . . ." Mark Van den Wijngaert, "La répression allemande en Belgique pendant la seconde guerre mondiale," in Van den Wijngaert et al., *Les bourreaux de Breendonk*, 11.

20 "Jews and dangerous prisoners": Steinberg and Schram, *Mechelen-Auschwitz*, 184.

"the elimination of . . .": Kogon, *Theory and Practice of Hell*, 20.

21 "a good Nazi": Nefors, *Breendonk 1940–1945*, 176.

3. FACING THE WALL
28 *Hier ist es kein Sanatorium*: Ochs, *Breendonck*, 28.

Ich sehe, ich höre alles!: Fischer, *L'enfer de Breendonck*, 71.

29 "expressive of depravity . . .": Ibid., 68.

30 *Bitte eintreten . . .*: Nefors, *Breendonk 1940–1945*, 46.

32 "I'm a tailor . . .": Interview with Jacques Frydman, National Memorial Fort Breendonk Archive.

4. THE FIRST PRISONERS OF ROOM 1
37 "the pig-man": Headquarters 21 Army Group, *Report*, 59.

38 "his beliefs and . . .": Nefors, *Breendonk 1940–1945*, 273.

39 "Who is a Jew here?" and following dialogue: Lévy, *Le défi, 1940*, 62.

40 "not to the Germans' taste": National Archives of Belgium, Section 5, "Archives contemporaines," Abraham Feldberg, Rapport, Ville d'Arlon, 8 July 1949.

5. THE ARTIST OF ROOM 1
43 *Nummer 56 meldet* . . . and following dialogue: Ochs, *Breendonck*, 64.

6. WATCHING THE PRISONERS
51 "I will bring you . . .": Interview with Jacques Frydman, National Memorial Fort Breendonk Archive.

7. THE *ZUGFÜHRER* OF ROOM 1
55 "Oh . . . you have . . .": Nefors, *Breendonk 1940–1945*, 248.

"who considered it . . .": Piens, *La vie des postiers*, 89.

"Here you . . .": Lévy, *Le défi*, 67.

8. A DAY AT BREENDONK

62 "his bed, a shapeless . . .": Ochs, *Breendonck*, 38.

65 "heavy work for . . .": Wager, "Breendonk 30 Years After the War," C21.

68 "lying on their cot . . .": Ochs, *Breendonck*, 36–37.

69 "All this seemed . . .": Nefors, *Breendonk 1940–1945*, 27.

9. CHANGES

74 "to be submissive . . .": Lévy, *Le défi*, 92.

75 "*Für mich, um krank . . .*": Ochs, *Breendonck*, 58.

10. THE FIRST ESCAPE

80 "bronchopneumonia and heart failure": Vander Velpen, *Breendonk*, 37.

81 "You don't have . . .": Interview with Jacques Frydman, National Memorial Fort Breendonk Archive.

"It was Prauss . . .": Headquarters 21 Army Group, *Report*, 52.

11. DESPAIR

85 "As soon as . . .": Goube, "Testimony of an Escaped Prisoner," 2.

86 "Just throw it . . .": National Memorial Fort Breendonk Archive, Wilchar Room 5.

"the guy jumped . . .": Ibid.

"Fifteen days later . . .": Ibid.

87 "waiting for the right moment . . .": Ochs, *Breendonck*, 45.

"The day will come . . .": Board of Directors, Fort of Breendonk, 63–64.

"special recommendation": Lévy, "Breendonck," 152.

88 "he devoured in less . . .": Ibid.

"natural death": Vander Velpen, *Breendonk*, 38.

90 "I cannot remember . . .": *La cité nouvelle*, "Des détenus ont été battus," 1.

12. A PICTURE-PERFECT CAMP

92 "Jews and non-Belgian prisoners": Lévy, "Présentation," 5.

96 "for the crime . . .": Fischer, *L'Enfer de Breendonck*, 74.

"For the last time . . .": Peeraer, "'t Gruwelkamp Breendonk."

13. OPERATION SOLSTICE

103 "a driving force . . .": Pahaut and Maerten, *Le fort de Breendonk*, 39.

14. PRISONER NUMBER 59

106 "clumsy and simple-minded": Ochs, *Breendonck*, 34.

107 "lying on the pavement . . .": Ibid.

108 "A villain tried . . .": Ibid., 47–48.

"If any among . . .": Fischer, *L'enfer de Breendonck*, 58.

"completely naked . . .": Ochs, *Breendonck*, 48.

109 "Look . . .": Goube, "Testimony of an Escaped Prisoner," 3.

"You see . . .": Fischer, *L'enfer de Breendonck*, 59.

15. A SUBSTITUTION

112 "Your father . . ." and following dialogue: Lasareff, *La vie remporta la victoire*, 15.

113 "Have you gone . . .": Ibid., 16.

"I knew nothing . . .": Ibid., 17–18.

114 "It was my . . .": Ibid., 18.

115 "One forty-one, why aren't . . ." and following dialogue: Ibid., 26.

16. THE RIVALS

120 "Sir sentry . . .": Headquarters 21 Army Group, *Report*, 32.

121 "You are only . . .": Lévy, *Le défi*, 96.

"You, the pure . . .": Ibid.

"Divide. Prevail . . .": Ibid., 97.

"who, dragging his . . .": Fischer, *L'enfer de Breendonck*, 104.

"wore the distinctive . . .": Ibid.

122   "Can a Jewish . . ." and following dialogue: Ibid.
        "without thirty-one . . .": Lévy, *Le défi*, 94.
        "For them, that . . .": Ibid.

17. THE PLANT EATERS
125   "hungry from every . . .": Lévy, *Le défi*, 89.
126   "It will fit . . .": Bamps, *De lijdensweg van Louis Bamps*.
        "hollow cheeks . . .": Solonevitch, *Breendonck*, 66.
128   "Why did you . . ." and following dialogue: Henderickx, *Les mémoires d'un prisonnier politique*, 38–39.
129   "inflammation of the . . .": Nefors, *Breendonk, 1940–1945*, 23.
        "Blinded by hunger . . .": Henderickx, *Les mémoires d'un prisonnier politique*, 36–37.
131   "Which one of . . ." and following conversation: Lévy, *Le défi*, 90.

18. JULY 24, 1941
134   "ranting and raving . . .": Bamps, *De lijdensweg van Louis Bamps*.
135   "was used as . . .": Headquarters 21 Army Group, *Report*, 32.
137   "Will you stand . . .": Lasareff, *La vie remporta la victoire*, 29.
        "Herr Lieutenant . . .": Ibid.
138   "He looks like . . .": Ochs, *Breendonck*, 43.

19. THE HELL OF BREENDONK
141   "fixed his eyes . . .": Solonevitch, *Breendonck*, 61.
        "[If] he continued to . . ." and following dialogue: Ibid., 60.
143   "an extended stay . . .": Nefors, *Breendonk 1940–1945*, 66.
        "sunken eyes glowed . . .": Ochs, *Breendonck*, 59.
        "Suddenly, in front . . .": Ibid.

20. THE FIRST TRANSPORT
147   "The man could . . .": Blommaert, *Breendonk: Toen ze baas in Eigen Kamp waren*.

149   "like toads": Henderickx, *Les mémoires d'un prisonnier politique*, 59.
151   "How is it . . .": Ibid., 63.

21. A TEMPORARY LULL
154   "Are you able . . ." and following dialogue: Lévy, *Le défi*, 109.
156   "a physical ruin": Somerhausen, *Written in Darkness*, 126.
158   "SS guardian angel": Ochs, *Breendonck*, 78.
        "the long tunnel . . .": Ibid., 79.

22. THE *SAMMELLAGER* IN MECHELEN
167   "would receive a . . .": Schreiber, *Twentieth Train*, 58.
168   "Does she still . . .": Kazerne Dossin Archive, Charlotte Hamburger correspondence.
170   "the waiting room . . .": M. Meckl, as quoted in De Prins, "De Gevangen van het Auffanlager Breendonk, 1940–1944," 52.

23. TRANSPORT II TO AUSCHWITZ-BIRKENAU
172   "massive, organized, and . . .": Dorien Styven (personal communication, 7 June 2013).
174   "a work order . . .": Steinberg and Schram, *Mecheln-Auschwitz*, 208.
176   "Dear Mama, Dad . . .": Kazerne Dossin Archive, Charlotte Hamburger correspondence.
177   "Dear Mama, Grandmother . . .": Ibid.
        "Having been persecuted . . .": National Archives of Belgium, Section 5, "Archives contemporaines," Mozes Weissbart, 4 July 1939.
181   "an SS doctor . . .": Piper, "Gas Chambers and Crematoria," 162.
183   "It is five . . .": Auschwitz-Birkenau Memorial and Museum, Belgium exhibit.
184   "displayed a clear . . .": Steinberg and Schram, *Mecheln-Auschwitz*, 226.

24. THE POSTAL WORKERS OF BRUSSELS

190 "sabotage the censor": Gysermans, *Des postiers prisonniers politiques rescapés,* 43.

191 "the lack of . . .": Piens, *La vie des postiers dans l'enfer de Breendonk,* 51.

193 "I will teach . . .": Klieger, "'J'apprendrai aux Juis,'" 2.

"This is Hell . . .": Interview with Georges De Bleser, National Memorial Fort Breendonk Archive.

"Your finger or . . .": SS office, National Memorial Fort Breendonk Archive.

"Breendonk within Breendonk": Nefors, *Breendonk 1940–1945,* 256.

"There was no . . .": Headquarters 21 Army Group, *Report,* 72.

195 "I will teach . . .": and following dialogue: Gysermans, *Des postiers prisonniers politiques rescapés,* 75–76.

197 "died of lung . . .": Nefors, *Breendonk 1940–1945,* 134.

25. THE FIRST EXECUTIONS

199 "Let me know . . .": Papers of Louis De Houwer, courtesy Albertine De Houwer.

200 "Soon it will . . .": Ibid.

"sweater you sent . . .": Ibid.

"that her dad . . .": Ibid.

201 "Just the right . . .": Van Daele, "Zo Was Het on Breendonk en Buchenwald."

202 "Give me a . . .": Ibid.

26. THE *ARRESTANTEN*

205 "like a dog . . .": Statement from prisoner Joseph Pia, National Memorial Fort Breendonk Archive.

206 "Do you want . . ." and following dialogue: Ibid.

207 "walking skeletons . . .": English Audio Guide, 17, National Memorial Fort Breendonk Archive.

208 "Are you a . . .": Ibid.

210 "What color was . . .": Ibid., 59.

212 "Does he know . . .": Ibid., 68.

27. THE BUNKER

215 "You will talk . . .": [Jospa], "Notes biographiques," National Memorial Fort Breendonk Archive.

216 "DEATH TO SS . . .": Améry, *At the Mind's Limits,* 24.

"twisted noses . . .": Ibid., 25.

217 "If you talk . . .": Ibid., 26.

"its own anesthetic . . .": Ibid., 29.

"prison, interrogation . . .": Ibid., 25.

"Now it's . . .": Ibid., 32.

218 "a crackling and . . .": Améry, *At the Mind's Limits,* 32–33.

221 "It's easy to . . .": Wager, "Breendonk 30 Years After the War," C21.

"intended to . . .": Headquarters 21 Army Group, *Report,* 33.

222 "It's no good . . .": Ibid.

"punches and truncheon . . .": Ibid.

"[Every day] I am still . . .": Améry, *At the Mind's Limits,* 36.

28. JANUARY 6, 1943

224 "You'll get to . . .": Trido, *Breendonck,* 21.

225 "the noise of . . .": Ibid., 23.

"So ended the . . .": Ibid., 24.

226 "In their minds . . .": Ibid., 31.

"the cleverest, meanest . . .": Somerhausen, *Written in Darkness,* 204.

227 "Resist the Nazi . . .": Steinberg and Schram, *Mecheln-Auschwitz,* 210.

228 "the dastardly . . .": *Brüsseler Zeitung,* quoted in De Prins, "De Gevangen van het Auffanlager Breendonk, 1940–1944," 119.

"abandoned their . . .": "Arnaud Fraiteur," National Memorial Fort Breendonk Archive.

29. THE WINTER OF 1942–43

231 "real beast": Gysermans, *Des postiers prisonniers politiques rescapés,* 94.

"Nothing could be . . .": Trido, *Breendonck,* 37.

232 "depression and weak . . .": Steinberg and Schram, *Mecheln-Auschwitz,* 191.

232 "I had a . . .": National Archives of Belguim, Section 5, "Archives contemporaines," Hugo Schönagel, 29 May 1938.
233 "You can't work . . ." and following dialogue: Trido, *Breendonck,* 83–84.

30. TRANSPORT XX
238 "shot on arrival": Schreiber, *Twentieth Train,* 223.
"Get out . . .": Transport XX, Mechelen—Boortmeerbeek—Auschwitz, 19 April 1943, "Robert Maistriau."
"A man from the . . .": Transport XX, Mechelen—Boortmeerbeek—Auschwitz, 19 April 1943, "Hena Wasyng."
239 "Put your hands": Schreiber, *Twentieth Train,* 228
240 "Get out . . .": Landau, *Flucht aus Wien,* 10.
"Can you walk?" and following dialogue: Ibid.
241 "So far you've . . .": Schreiber, *Twentieth Train,* 216.
"Yes, sir" and following dialogue: Landau, *Flucht aus Wien,* 10.

31. THE CHAPLAIN OF THE EXECUTIONS
243 "They came to . . .": Trido, *Breendonck,* 79.
245 "all of them . . .": *La cité nouvelle,* "Parce que les condamnés à mort chantaient," 1.
"makes a very . . .": Diary of Otto Gramman, 14 July 1943, National Memorial Fort Breendonk Archives.
"They have to . . .": Ibid.
"the condemned men": *La cité nouvelle,* 4 April 1946, 1.
246 "Long live the . . ." and following dialogue: Diary of Otto Gramman, 14 July 1943, National Memorial Fort Breendonk Archives.
"All of them . . .": Ibid.
"did not even . . .": Stippelmans, *Mijn Verhaal, Razzia te Sint-Truiden, 1943–45.*
247 "were just implementers . . .": Nefors, *Breendonk 1940–1945,* 162.
"was at times . . .": Ibid.

247 "Ready, set, fire!": Ibid.
"and the shootings . . .": Nefors, *Breendonk 1940–1945,* 163.

32. TWO HEROES OF BREENDONK
249 "Now you know . . .": Lévy, "L'hallucinante histoire d'un bourreau de Breendonck," 1.
250 "coffee, a jar . . .": Schreiber, *Twentieth Train,* 249.
"For two hours . . .": Ibid., 249–50.
251 "Even if words . . .": Letter from Youra Livchitz to his mother, National Memorial Fort Breendonk Archives.
252 "They both died . . .": Schreiber, *Twentieth Train,* 251.

33. THE TWELVE FROM SENZEILLES
254 "arms and ammunition . . .": Somerhausen, *Written in Darkness,* 168.
255 "These hangings . . .": Tielemans, *Van boerenzoon tot politieke gevangene.*
256 "DEATH SENTENCE AND . . .": "Condemnation à mort et exécution de 12 terroristes," National Memorial Fort Breendonk Archives.
"autopsy revealed that . . .": Ibid.
257 "acknowledged . . . 633 acts . . .": Pahaut and Maerten, *Le fort de Breendonk,* 57.

34. EVACUATING BREENDONK
263 "I see him . . .": Bert Van Hoorick, quoted in Nefors, *Breendonk 1940–1945,* 259–60.
"I rushed him . . ." and following dialogue: Nefors, *Breendonk, 1940–1945,* 257.
264 "execution posts . . .": "The Liberation of Antwerp, 4 September 1944" [Major Brice Somers], National Memorial Fort Breendonk Archives.
"seemed to be . . .": Ibid.
265 "Collaborators are locked . . .": Van der Auwera, "Auffanglager Breendonk."

266 "anyone suspected of . . .": Pahaut and Maerten, *Le fort de Breendonk,* 11.

35. JOURNEY FROM MAUTHAUSEN
268 "He pointed . . .": Dubois, 1940–1945 Waarom.
271 "running with . . .": Ibid.

36. END OF THE SUPERMEN
277 "But you're SS . . ." and following dialogue: Landau, "The First Days of Freedom," 80.
"The liberators are . . .": Landau, "Man Versus Supermen," 130.
"Tell your people . . .": Landau, "The First Days of Freedom," 80.
278 "A feeling of resistance . . .": Landau, "Man Versus Supermen," 130.
"Forgotten are hunger . . .": Ibid., 132.
"starved, liberated people . . .": Ibid.
279 "the most moving . . .": Landau, "The First Days of Freedom," 82.

37. THE FINAL TRANSPORT FROM NEUENGAMME
281 "was man's . . .": Meier, "Holzauge sei wachsam."
282 "in his wooden . . .": Ibid.
"his sprightly . . .": Ibid.
284 "In the name . . .": National Archives, United Kingdom, WO 235/162.
285 "The first smoke-trailing . . .": Jacobs and Pool, *100-Year Secret: Britain's Hidden World War II Massacre,* 102.

38. THE WAR CRIMES TRIALS
292 "quiet and industrious . . .": Lévy, "Dans deux ou trois mois, le procès de Breendonck pourra s'ouvrir," 1.
"saw tears flow . . .": Lévy, "L'hallucinante histoire d'un bourreau de Breendonck," 4.
"a victim of . . .": Ibid.
293 "extinguished his cigarette . . .": Klieger, "Un jour je te tuerai, cochon!," 1.

294 "I still do . . .": *La cité nouvelle,* "Le verdict sera rendu le 7 mai," 3.
295 "We do not . . .": Dimitri Roden, "Les bourreaux devant leurs juges," in Van den Wijngaert et al., *Les bourreaux de Breendonk,* 147.
297 "ten bullets hit . . .": Ibid., 152.

39. THE FINAL DEATH
299 "Take off your . . .": and following dialogue: Nefors, *Breendonk 1940–1945,* 185.
"Oh, I can stand . . .": Vander Velpen, *Breendonk,* 238.
300 "As far as I . . ." and following dialogue: Ibid., 242–43.
301 "of 57 murders . . .": Laurence Schram, *Transit Camp for Jews in Mechelen.*
302 "to comply with . . .": *New York Times,* "Belgians Protest Pro-Nazi Clemency," 10.
"expressed absolutely no . . .": Vander Velpen, *Breendonk,* 246.

40. BREENDONK TODAY
303 "For four long . . .": Lévy, "Breendonck," 160.

BIBLIOGRAPHY

BOOKS, REPORTS, AND DOCUMENTS

Adriaens, Ward, Maxime Steinberg, and Laurence Schram. *Mecheln-Auschwitz, 1942–1944*. Vols. 1–4. Brussels: VUBPress, 2009.

Améry, Jean. *At the Mind's Limits: Contemplations by a Survivor on Auschwitz and Its Realities*. Translated by Sidney Rosenfeld and Stella P. Rosenfeld. New York: Schocken Books, 1986.

Arblaster, Paul. *A History of the Low Countries*. 2nd ed. New York: Palgrave Macmillan, 2012.

Die Ausstellungen: KZ-Gedenkstätte Neuengamme. Bremen, Germany: Edition Temmen, 2005.

Bamps, Louis. *De lijdensweg van Louis Bamps, KULTUR? Politiek gevange Breendonk, Hoei, Antwerpen*. www.getuigen.be (accessed 7 September, 2013).

Bitton-Jackson, Livia. *I Have Lived a Thousand Years*. New York: Simon Pulse, 1999.

Blommaert, Thomas. *Breendonk: Toen ze baas in Eigen Kamp waren*. Uitpers: Webzine voor Internationale Politiek, No. 47, archief.uitpers.be (accessed 29 April 2014).

Board of Directors of Fort Breendonk Memorial. *The Fort of Breendonk*.

Buch, P., R. Linthout, and F. Selleslagh. *Breendonk: Les débuts*. Brussels: CEGES, 1997.

Cornet, Jose. *Demain le soleil: De la Gestapo aux camps de la mort*. Brussels: J. M. Collet, 1987.

De Prins, Gert. "De Gevangen van het Auffanglager Breendonk, 1940–1944: Toelichting bij de Herziene Namenlijst." Unpublished report, November 7, 2008.

Dubois, Jean. 1940–1945 Waarom. www.getuigen.be (accessed 20 June 2013).

Feig, Konnilyn G. *Hitler's Death Camps: The Sanity of Madness*. New York: Holmes & Meier, 1981.

Fischer, Frans. *L'enfer de Breendonck. Souvenirs vécus*. Brussels: Editions Labor, 1944.

Friedlander, Henry. *The Origins of Nazi Genocide*. Chapel Hill: University of North Carolina Press, 1995.

Fulbrook, Mary. *A Small Town Near Auschwitz: Ordinary Nazis and the Holocaust*. Oxford: Oxford University Press, 2012.

Goube, Pierre. "Testimony of an Escaped Prisoner from Germany." John LaFarge, SJ, Papers, GTMGamms69, Georgetown University Library Special Collections Research Center, Washington, D.C.

Gysermans, Jules. *Des postiers prisonniers politiques rescapés, Der postmannen politieke gevangen ontsnapten: Album-Souvenir de Breendonk*. Brussels: n.d.

Headquarters 21 Army Group. *Report on German Atrocities*. December 1944.

Heidelberger-Leonard, Irène. *The Philosopher of Auschwitz: Jean Améry and Living with the Holocaust*. London: I. B. Tauris, 2010.

Henderickx, Adrien. *Les mémoires d'un prisonnier politique: Breendonk, Neuengamme, 1940–1945*. St. Pieters Leeuw, Belgium: Adrien Henderickx, n.d.

Hoyaux, Gaston. *32 mois sous la matraque des S.S.* Brussels: Editions Labor, 1945.

Jacob, Simon. *Les sept de Mons*. Brussels/Willebroek: Buch Edition and Memorial Breendonk, 2005.

Jacobs, Benjamin, and Eugene Pool. *The 100-Year Secret: Britain's Hidden World War II Massacre.* Guildford, Conn.: Lyons Press, 2004.

Kogon, Eugen. *The Theory and Practice of Hell: The German Concentration Camps and the System Behind Them.* Translated by Heinz Norden. New York: Farrar, Straus and Giroux, 2006.

Landau, Ernest. "The First Days of Freedom." In *After the Holocaust: Rebuilding Jewish Lives in Postwar Germany,* edited by Michael Brenner. Translated by Barbara Harshav. Princeton: Princeton University Press, 1997.

_____. *Flucht aus Wien.* Unpublished manuscript.

_____. "Man Versus Supermen." In *The Root and the Bough: The Epic of an Enduring People,* edited by Leo W. Schwarz. New York: Rinehart & Company, 1949: 127–132.

Lasareff, Vladimir. *La vie remporta la victoire.* Paris, 1945.

Lévy, Paul M. G. "Breendonck." In *Héros et martyrs: 1940–1945, Les fusillés.* Brussels: Editions J. Rosez, 1946.

_____. *Le défi, 1940: Le refus, l'epreuve et le combat.* Brussels: Vie Ouvrière, 1985.

_____. "Présentation." In *Breendonk: Les débuts,* by P. Buch, R. Linthout, and F. Selleslagh. Brussels: CEGES, 1997.

"Manifest Markings; Reading the Record of Detained Aliens." www.jewishgen. org (accessed 13 October 2013).

Mannheimer, Max. "Theresienstadt—Auschwitz—Warsaw—Dachau: Recollections." In *Dachau and Nazi Terror 1933–1945,* edited by Wolfgang Benz and Barbara Distel. Volume 1: *Testimonies and Memoirs.* Dachau, Germany: Dachauer Hefte, 2002.

Megargee, Geoffrey P., ed. *Encyclopedia of Camps and Ghettos, 1933–1945.* Volume 1. Parts A and B. Bloomington: Indiana University Press, 2009.

Meier, Heinrich Christian. "Holzauge sei wachsam." Hamburg: Staatsarchiv. 622-1/216

Meinen, Insa. *La Shoah en Belgique.* Translated by Sylvaine Gillot-Soreau. Waterloo, Belgium: Renaissance du Livre, 2012.

Michman, Don, ed. *Belgium and the Holocaust: Jews, Belgians, Germans.* Jerusalem: Yad Vashem, 1998.

Ministère de la Justice, Commission des Crimes de Guerre. *Les crimes de guerre commis sous l'occupation de la Belgique 1940–1945: Le Camp de Torture de Breendonk.* 2nd ed. Liège, Belgium: Georges Thone, 1949.

Mosier, John. *Hitler vs. Stalin: The Eastern Front, 1941–1945.* New York: Simon & Schuster, 2010.

Motz, Roger. *Belgium Unvanquished.* London: Lindsay Drummond, 1942.

Müller, Peter. *Rüstungswahn und menschliches Leid-Bewältigung und Erinnerung: Das Bunkergelände im Mühldorfer Hart.* Mühldorf am Inn, Germany: Heimatbund, 2012.

Nasser, Stephen, with Sherry Rosenthal. *My Brother's Voice: A Story Kept Secret over Fifty Years.* Las Vegas: Stephen Nasser, 2013.

Nefors, Patrick. *Breendonk 1940–1945.* Translated by Emmanuel Brutsaert and Walter Hilgers. Brussels: Editions Racine, 2004.

_____. "Paul Lévy." In *Nouvelle Biographie Nationale.* Brussels: Académie royale des sciences, des lettres et des beaux-arts de Belgique, 2010.

Ochs, Jacques. *Breendonck: Bagnards et bourreaux.* Brussels: Editions du Nord Albert Parmentier, 1947.

Pahaut, Claire, and Fabrice Maerten. *Le fort de Breendonk.* Brussels: Editions Racine, 2006.

Peeraer, Jef. "'t Gruwelkamp Breendonk, Doorleefde Nachtmerries." www. getuigen.be (accessed 14 December 2013).

Piens, Désiré. *La vie des postiers dans l'enfer de Breendonk.* Brussels: 1947.

Piper, Franciszek. "Gas Chambers and Crematoria." In *Anatomy of the Auschwitz Death Camp,* edited by Yisrael Gutman and Michael Berenbaum. Bloomington: Indiana University Press, 1998: 157–82.

Pipes, Richard. *Communism.* New York: Modern Library, 2003.

Proceedings of a Military Court for the Trial of War Criminals Held at the Curio Haus, Hamburg. Kew, England, National Archives. WO 235/162.

Rosengarten, Israel K. *Survival: The Story of a Sixteen-Year-Old Jewish Boy.* Syracuse: Syracuse University Press, 1999.

Roth, Chaya. *The Fate of Holocaust Memories: Transmission and Family Dialogues.* Chicago: Chaya Roth, 2008.

Schleunes, Karl A. *The Twisted Road to Auschwitz: Nazi Policy Toward German Jews 1933–1939.* Urbana: University of Illinois Press, 1990.

Schram, Laurence. *The Transit Camp for Jews in Mechelen: The Antechamber of Death.* Online Encyclopedia of Mass Violence, www.massviolence.org (accessed 19 October 2013).

Schreiber, Marion. *The Twentieth Train: The True Story of the Ambush of the Death Train to Auschwitz.* Translated by Shaun Whiteside. New York: Grove Press, 2003.

Schwartz, Leslie, and Marc David Bonagura. *Surviving the Hell of Auschwitz and Dachau: A Teenage Struggle Toward Freedom from Hatred.* Zurich: Lit, 2013.

Smith, Marian L. "Manifest Markings: A Guide to Interpreting Passenger List Annotations." jewishgen.org (accessed 7 October 2013).

Sofsky, Wolfgang. *The Order of Terror: The Concentration Camp.* Translated by William Templer. Princeton: Princeton University Press, 1997.

Solonevitch, Boris. *Breendonck: Camp de tortures et de mort.* Brussels: Goemaere, 1944.

Somerhausen, Anne. *Written in Darkness: A Belgian Woman's Record of the Occupation 1940–1945.* New York: Alfred A. Knopf, 1946.

Steinberg, Maxime, and Laurence Schram. *Mecheln-Auschwitz: The Destruction of the Jews and Gypsies from Belgium, 1942–1944.* Vol. 4 of *Mecheln-Auschwitz, 1942–1944,* edited by Ward Adriaens, Maxime Steinberg, Laurence Schram, Eric Hautermann, and Patricia Ramet. Brussels: VUBPress, 2009.

Stengers, Jean. "Belgium." In *The European Right: A Historical Profile,* edited by Hans Rogger and Eugen Webe. Berkeley: University of California Press, 1966.

Stipplemans, Pierre. *Mijn verhaal, Razzia te Sint-Truiden, 1943–1945.* www.getuigen.be (accessed 26 October 2013).

Styven, Dorien. E-mail message to author, 7 June 2013.

Tielemans, Jules. *Van boerenzoon tot politieke gevangene: Het verhaal over Albert Tielemans.* PowerPoint presentation, n.d.

Trepper, Leopold. *The Great Game: Memoirs of the Spy Hitler Couldn't Silence.* New York: McGraw-Hill, 1977.

Trido, Victor. *Breendonck: Le camp du silence, de la mort et du crime.* Charleroi, Belgium, 1944.

Van Daele, Karel. "Zó was het Breendonk en in Buchenwald." www.getuigen.be (accessed 27 May 2013).

Van den Wijngaert, Mark, Dimitri Roden, and Tine Jorissen. *Auffanglager Breendonk 1940–1944: De gevangenen van Breendonk Gedenkboek/ Les prisonniers de Breendonk: Livre-Mémorial.* Willebroek, Belgium: Print House of Defense, 2012

Van den Wijngaert, Mark, et al. *Les bourreaux de Breendonk*. Translated by Emmanuel Brutsaert and Walter Hilgers. Brussels: Editions Racine, 2012.

Van der Auwera, Gerd."Auffanglager Breendonk." Go2war2.nl (accessed 20 September 2012).

Vander Velpen, Jos. *Breendonk: Chronique d'un camp (1940–1944)*. Brussels: Editions Aden, 2004.

Van Goethem, Herman. *Holocaust and Human Rights*. Mechelen, Belgium: Kazerne Dossin, 2012.

Von Fraunberg, Bero, and Renate. *Damals im April: Chronologie zum Seeshaupter Mahnmal*. Seeshaupt, Germany: SeeshaupterAnsammlungen, 2010.

Wachsman, Nicolas. *Hitler's Prisons: Legal Terror in Nazi Germany*. New Haven: Yale University Press, 2004.

Wasserstein, Bernard. *On the Eve: The Jews of Europe Before the Second World War*. New York: Simon and Schuster, 2012.

NEWSPAPERS

La cité nouvelle. "16 condamnations à mort." 8 May 1946, 1.

La cité nouvelle. "Des detenus ont été battus." 8 March 1946, 1.

La cité nouvelle. "Parce que les condamnés à mort chantaient." 4 April 1946, 1.

La cité nouvelle. "Le verdict sera rendu le 7 mai." 14–15 April 1946, 3.

Klieger, Bernard."'J'apprendrai aux Juifs à travailler, s'ils ne m'écoutent pas, je les tuerai!'" *La cité nouvelle* (Brussels), 5 April 1946, 1.

———."Un jour je te tuerai, cochon!" *La cité nouvelle* (Brussels), 20 March 1946, 1.

Lévy, Paul M.G."Breendonck!" *La cité nouvelle*, 8 May 1946, 1, 6.

———. "Dans deux ou trois mois, le procès de Breendonck pourra s'ouvrir." *La cité nouvelle*, 12 December 1945, 1.

———. "Deux documents nouveaux à mettre au dossier." *La cité nouvelle*, 3 April 1946, 1, 3.

———. "L'hallucinante histoire d'un bourreau de Breendonck." *La cité nouvelle*, 20–21 January 1946, 1, 4.

———. "J'ai temoigné devant les juges de mes bourreaux." *La cité nouvelle*, 8 March 1946, 1, 4.

———. "Le premier grand procès de Breendonck." *La cité nouvelle*, 5 March 1946, 1, 3.

Los Angeles Times. "Belgian Nazi Camp Still Festering Sore." 4 September 1977, B9.

New York Times. "Belgians Protest Pro-Nazi Clemency." 3 September 1952, 10.

De Volksgazet. "Walter Obler, de Joodsche Werkbaas te Breendonck, aange- houden." 29 November 1945, 3.

Wager, Richard. "Breendonk 30 Years After the War." *Chicago Tribune*, 1 June 1975, C21.

NATIONAL MEMORIAL FORT BREENDONK ARCHIVE

"Arnaud Fraiteur." Archive number 422.

"Condemnation à mort et exécution de 12 terroristes." Archive number 701.

Diary of Otto Gramman.

Interview with Georges De Bleser. Archive number 340.

Interview with Jacques Frydman. Archive number 349.

[Jospa, Ghert.] "Notes biographiques." Archive number 347.

[Klibanski, Isaac.] "Breendonck." Archive number 348.

Letter from Youra Livchitz to his mother. Archive number 286.
[Lévy, Paul M. G.] "Breendonk Concentration Camp." Archive number 138.
"Les rescapés de Breendonck viennent accuser leurs bourreaux." Archive number 388.
Statement from prisoner Edouard Franckx. SS office.
Statement from prisoner Joseph Pia. Archive number 557.
Statement from prisoner Wilhelm Pauwels. Room 5: Eating in the room.

NATIONAL ARCHIVES OF BELGIUM

Oscar Beck (1.613.798)
Abraham Feldberg (1.384.138)
Sacha Frenkel (7.307.583)
Willy Giersch (7.194.760)
Ludwig Juliusberger (7.238.856)
Herman Kahn (7.172.845)
Jacob Kiper (1.623.974)
Pavel Koussonsky (7.295.543)
Vladimir Lasareff (1.078.332)
Sally Lewin (7.335.573)
Mozes Louft (7.104.724)
Israel Neumann (1.478.427)
Herz Nisenholz (1.644.385)
Walter Obler (7.308.340)
Leo Schmandt (7.334.036)
Hugo Schönagel (7.300.015)
Israel Steinberg (7.021.310)
Eljasz Swirski (7.117.830)
Hirsz Swirski (7.095.551)
Mozes Weissbart (7.363.670)

DIRECTORATE-GENERAL WAR VICTIMS ARCHIVE

René Blieck
Louis De Houwer
Abraham Feldberg
Charlotte Hamburger
Ludwig Juliusberger
Jacob Kiper
Israel Neumann
Eleonore Sabathova
Albert Tielemans

ACKNOWLEDGMENTS

The day that I visited the National Memorial Fort Breendonk for the first time, I knew I wanted to write a book about it. A few months later, I made an appointment to meet with Dimitri Roden, the historian at the memorial. He welcomed me into his office on the second floor of the former camp and listened to an American writer discuss his ideas for a book about the camp. He not only encouraged me, but granted me complete access to the archives. I was able to spend two weeks there, reading and copying material, examining photos and drawings, and perhaps most important of all, conversing with Dimitri. His help at the beginning allowed me to build a good foundation of knowledge about the camp before proceeding.

I realized early on that *Auffanglager* Breendonk was inextricably connected to the SS *Sammellager* in Mechelen, especially after I came across information about Charlotte Hamburger and Louis De Houwer. Consequently, I met and frequently corresponded with Dorien Styven, assistant archivist at the Kazerne Dossin Museum Memorial and Documentation Centre on Holocaust and Human Rights, the former home of the *Sammellager*. Dorien kindly provided me with information about many Breendonk prisoners who were eventually transported from the camp and about the transports themselves. She also helped me contact Albertine De Houwer, the daughter of Charlotte Hamburger and Louis De Houwer. I couldn't have written the same book without Dorien's help.

Gert De Prins, archivist at the Department of War Victims in Brussels, and I developed a friendship during my first visit to his archive. I quickly learned that Breendonk was one of his interests as a historian. He very generously shared with me his own unpublished report about the prisoners at the camp. This valuable document summarized and analyzed the known statistics, including how the prisoners were numbered, how many died through illness, abuse, and execution, and how many escaped. We emailed frequently and met occasionally to discuss various aspects of the camp, including its many unsolved mysteries. I am very grateful for his help.

As I uncovered information, some brand new, some long lost, I came into contact with a number of other people who gave me helpful advice and support. Filip Strubbe of the National Archives of Belgium assisted me many times as I searched for immigration files of former Breendonk prisoners. Maude Henry, Benoit Labarre, and Thierry Dewin of the Royal Library of Belgium were also very helpful in my search for information and photographs about Breendonk. Alyn Beßmann, archivist at the Neuengamme Concentration Camp Memorial, received me without advance notice and provided me with many documents and photographs. Olivier Van der Wilt, the conservator of Breendonk, and Saskia De Vos, an archivist who replaced Dimitri Roden for a year, were very helpful in answering my many questions and in locating the all-important drawings of Jacques Ochs. And Phyllis Kramer of jewishgen.org offered me some needed advice as I researched Israel Neumann and his family.

Of course, during my many visits to Belgium, I spent time with Albertine De Houwer and her husband, Hugo Poppe, as well as Pierre Blieck and his family, and Jules Tielemans. I cannot thank them enough for sharing their family stories and photos with me so that I could give a fuller account of Louis De Houwer and Charlotte Hamburger, René Blieck, and Albert Tielemans. And Edi Landau, son of Ernest Landau, provided me with many unpublished works by his father.

Four people helped me with English translations. Professor Thomas Kovach, of the Department of German Studies at the University of Arizona, translated an entry from Otto Gramann's execution diary that was handwritten in Sudeten German. My Belgian friend Diane Vandepaepeliere translated postcards and letters written by Charlotte Hamburger and Louis De Houwer. The Neuengamme archivist Alyn Bessmann translated a letter that René Blieck wrote to his wife from Neuengamme. My good friend Juanita Havill helped with the translation of René Blieck's poem on page 287 and also offered much-needed moral support. I cannot thank them enough for their help. For better or worse, I provided the other English translations in the book of material written in French, Dutch, and German.

I am also very pleased to acknowledge and heartily thank Leon Nolis, a relatively new Belgian photographer, who was an amazing discovery for me. After I found online some photographs that he had taken of Breendonk, I emailed to ask if he would allow me to use them in this book. That first email mushroomed into a lasting friendship not only with Leon, but with his partner, Diane. Given total access to photograph Breendonk, Leon spent many days at the camp in all types of weather to pursue his art. His photographs convey the camp's very essence.

Finally, I would like to share one story

about my research process. Near the end of my work on the book, I made a quick trip to Munich to see where Ernest Landau (chapter 36) had been liberated in Germany. Although Landau had written two accounts of his liberation, specific information about the train and the funeral for the dead prisoners was fuzzy. I was especially confused about the location of the memorial for the prisoners: Was it in Seeshaupt or Tutzing?

So I flew into Munich one snowy Sunday morning in February 2014, rented a car, and drove south to Seeshaupt, where I found absolutely nothing. I had struck out. That same afternoon, I stopped at the concentration camp memorial site in Dachau to visit the bookshop, hoping to locate a book about the Mühldorf subcamp where Ernest Landau had been imprisoned before his final train ride and liberation. When I did not find anything, I asked the woman working in the shop, "Do you know anything about the train from Mühldorf that was bombed by Americans near Tutzing?"

The woman was Susanne von Loeffelholz. She showed me a book by a man who had been liberated from a train that had originated in Mühldorf but had been liberated in another town. How many evacuation trains, I wondered, had the Nazis sent from Mühldorf? Susanne did not know the answer, but she took my email address and promised to find out something and write.

This conversation with Susanne, and a subsequent email from her a few days after I arrived home, helped me think differently about the train, and so I refined my search. I went on to discover that a film had been made about the train, *Endstation Seeshaupt* (or "End of the Line, Seeshaupt"), written and directed by the German filmmaker Walter Steffen.

I wrote Steffen a brief email to ask if the Seeshaupt train was the same one that Ernest Landau had been on. He did not know (after all, he was not a historian, and there were thousands of prisoners on the train), but he sent me an Internet link so that I could watch his film online. The film informed me that the train had been divided in half; there had been two trains, and each had been liberated in a different town: Train 1 near Tutzing, Train 2 in Seeshaupt. Ernest Landau, I realized, had been on Train 1.

Walter Steffen also suggested that I contact a historian he had worked with while making the film. This man, Heinrich Mayer, who was a retired high school history teacher who lived in Munich, offered to take me on the route of the train if I returned to Germany. And so I did, on a very quick two-day trip, that April. Heinrich not only drove me along the train's route, but took me to the remains of the Mühldorf-Mettenheim airplane factory and the works' barracks. He introduced me to Edwin Hamberger, an archivist studying the Muhldorf camp; Renate von Fraunberg, a journalist who wrote a book about the liberation of Train 2 in Seeshaupt and who was instrumental in having a memorial to the prisoners erected there; and Michaela Pischetsrieder, who escorted us to the place where Ernest Landau's train had been liberated and the field (actually a new cemetery at the time) where the dead prisoners were originally buried. I had the details that the chapter had been missing, and all because I asked Susanne von Loeffelholz a question in the Dachau bookstore.

As Susanne told me, "I do not believe in coincidences."

Neither do I.

And so I want to thank finally Susanne von Loeffelholz, Walter Steffen, Edwin Hamberger, Renate von Fraunberg, Michaela Pischetsrieder, and, most of all, Heinrich Mayer, who took me on an unforgettable journey.

When you are working on a complicated project and ask questions in your pursuit of the truth, all kinds of amazing connections can occur. Such moments happened over and over again as I researched the prisoners in the book; this was just the final example.

Now that it is finished, I hope you can make your own connections from it as you take your own journey, no matter where it leads you.
— James M. Deem

Heinrich Mayer walks across the ruins of the Mühldorf aircraft factory.

ILLUSTRATION CREDITS

Archiv der KZ-Gedenkstaette Mauthausen (courtesy of Vaclav Berdych): 267

Archiv der KZ-Gedenkstaette Mauthausen (courtesy of SPB): 269

© Collections CEGES/SOMA, Brussels: 186, 188, 192, 248

© James M. Deem: xii, 4, 146, 179, 180, 261, 273, 277, 279, 287, 303, 334

© Directorate-General War Victims, Brussels: iii (second), iii (sixth), 103 (bottom), 172 (right), 195 (top), 196, 216

© Fort Breendonk: 17, 22, 38, 41, 44, 45 (top right), 88, 138, 140, 149, 152, 193, 230 (top), 233, 249, 297, 298, 307

© Gazet van Antwerpen: 291, 300

© Gemeentebestuur Willebroek: 184

© Kazerne Dossin, Mechelen: 162, 164, 167, 173, 175, 176, 183, 203

© Kazerne Dossin—Fonds Kummer, Mechelen: 171

© KIK-IRPA, Brussels: 45 (top left), 87

© Otto Kropf/Collection Otto Spronk/SOMA: 20, 25, 28, 47, 53, 56, 63, 65, 66, 91, 94, 95, 97, 115, 122, 123, 135, 142

Library of Congress USZ62-22339: 11

© National Archives of Belgium (Aliens' Police. Individual Files): iii (first), iii (third), iii (fifth), iii (eighth), 9, 12, 30, 36, 37, 39, 40, 45 (bottom), 49, 50, 54, 58, 73, 74, 80, 81, 89 (top right), 102, 103 (top), 106, 107, 110, 112, 134, 143, 156, 157, 172 (top left), 172 (bottom left), 177, 230 (bottom), 232, 312, 313, 314, 315, 317, 318

© Neuengamme Memorial: 150 (F1981-743), 280 (F1996-761), 283 (F1981-114), 286 (F1995-1280)

© Leon Nolis: i, 6–7, 13, 21, 24, 31, 34, 59, 60, 61, 62, 70–71, 72, 77, 98–99, 120, 124, 126, 160–61, 169, 186–87, 202, 204, 206, 208, 209, 211, 213, 214, 218, 219, 220, 223, 228, 229, 240, 242, 253, 258–59, 288–89, 304, 305, 308, 310–11, 336

Private Collection: 8, 18 (top), 165, 251

© Royal Library of Belgium. All Rights Reserved: 42, 46, 51, 57, 67, 69, 78, 79, 84, 127, 130, 131, 133, 136, 139, 154, 207

© SNCB, Brussels (with permission of Kazerne Dossin, Mechelen): 178

© Hans Peter Sørensen, Neuengamme Erindringer—20 Tegninger af Graenseovergendarm Hans P. Sørensen, Sønderborg o. J. (1946): 151

© Stadsarchief Mechelen: 235, 290, 294, 296, 301

© State Archives, Brussels: 166

© Jules Tielemans: 256

© United States Holocaust Memorial Museum (courtesy of Eugene S. Cohen): 271

© United States Holocaust Memorial Museum (courtesy of Paul Hartman): iii (second), 197 (left), 221, 222, 264

© United States Holocaust Memorial Museum (courtesy of Ilona Schecter): 270, 276

Today, this somber plaque mounted near the entrance tunnel announces that the national memorial of Fort Breendonk was unanimously created by an act of the Belgian parliament on August 19, 1947, in order to promote "the civic spirit of the nation and…the patriotic education of youth."

INDEX

Page numbers in **bold** type denote illustrations and photos.